INTEGRATED KEYBOARDING
COMMUNICATION SKILLS
Second Edition

Rosanne Reiff, Ph.D.
New York City
Board of Education

WC10BB
PUBLISHED BY
SOUTH-WESTERN PUBLISHING CO.
CINCINNATI, OH   WEST CHICAGO, IL   DALLAS, TX   LIVERMORE, CA

Preface

Integrated Keyboarding/Communication Skills has been designed to provide students with the communications skills that are essential in order to succeed in today's world of work.

■ Although office equipment may become obsolete from one year to another, the need for people with language arts skills remains unchanged. Today's equipment may be "smart"; however, the person who keyboards must use correct spelling, grammar, and punctuation in order for the finished product to be acceptable or mailable. The spoken word is just as important: those with poor grammatical skills have difficulty traveling along the road to success.

■ Especially because of the speed and huge reproductive capability of today's equipment, keyboarders must also possess a supplementary skill: the ability to proofread and recognize errors. Conversely, the keyboarder also should be able to indicate changes and/or corrections with proper proofreader's marks.

■ Finally, in processing materials, the keyboarder must be able to think—to make decisions and use judgment—rather than simply copy.

Integrated Keyboarding/Communication Skills provides instruction in all these areas with accompanying assignments in the form of personal notes, personal-business letters, and short reports. Some assignments are in script; some are in rough-draft form. New in this edition are proofreading assignments and context exercises, and there is a separate test packet. Review units appear after the third, sixth, ninth, and twelfth units.

DESCRIPTION OF LEARNING UNITS

The text contains 12 learning units. The exercises and assignments therein have been deliberately kept simple but relevant in order to retain students' interest in the primary matter at hand: improvement of language arts skills. The units are not cumulative; the assignments in each unit are based solely upon the principles taught in that unit. Each of the learning units contains the following sections:

1. *Principles to be Learned.* Each principle is fully explained and is followed by sample sentences and a try-out exercise.

2. *Sentence Exercise.* The student is to rekey each of the ten sentences in the spaces provided, making the necessary corrections.

3. *Dictionary Usage.* The more difficult words that appear in the keyboarding assignments are listed with their meanings, followed by ten sentences. After a review of the words and their meanings, the student is to complete each sentence, inserting in each blank the word from the list that best fits.

4. *Keyboarding Assignments*

A. Helpful-Hint Letter. This may be a personal note or personal business letter. The student is given a "hint" as to the number of times each principle that has been taught in the unit is used improperly or has been omitted. The student is to make the necessary corrections while keyboarding. Complete instructions for keyboarding the note or letter are given, including style, punctuation, margins, tabs, and placement of various letter parts. Most of the notes and letters are to be keyboarded line for line.

B. You're on Your Own. This section contains two assignments: a combination of a personal note, a personal-business letter, or a short report. The report appears in rough-draft form in every other unit. There are no hints as to the number of times various principles from the unit are improperly used or have been omitted. The student is to make the necessary corrections while keyboarding. Complete instructions are given, including style, punctuation, margins, tabs, and placement of various letter parts. Most of the assignments are to be keyboarded line for line.

C. Proofreading Assignment. The student is to indicate corrections in a short paragraph by inserting proofreader's marks.

D. Context Check. This exercise tests the student's understanding of the contents of the three keyboarding assignments in each unit. The student is to complete mostly open-ended sentences concerning each of the assignments.

REVIEW LESSON

Review lessons appear after the third, sixth, ninth, and twelfth units. Each review lesson is based on the principles learned in the previous three units. Each lesson consists of a 15-sentence exercise; two keyboarding assignments that include a personal note and either a report or personal-business letter (no instructions are provided for margin and tab sets and placement of various parts); and a proofreading review in which corrections are to be indicated in a short paragraph by the insertion of proofreader's marks.

TEST PACKET

Integrated Keyboarding/Communication Skills now contains a separate test packet for the teacher.

TEACHER'S MANUAL

The instructor's manual that accompanies *Integrated Keyboarding/Communications Skills* provides teaching suggestions, answer keys for the textbook exercises and assignments, methodology for the various sections of each unit, and suggestions for evaluation and grading.

Rosanne Reiff

Contents

4 Homonyms 37

5 Commas 47

6 Commas (concluded) 57

Review Lesson Units 4–6 66

7 Colon and Semicolon 71

8 The Apostrophe 83

9 Troublesome Words 93

Review Lesson Units 7-9 103

10 Troublesome Words (continued) 109

11 Numbers 119

12 Quotation Marks 129

Review Lesson Units 10-12 139

Reference Guide 144

Index 151

1 Capitalization

Upon completion of this unit, you will be able to apply capitalization-usage rules in written communications.

1-1 FIRST WORD OF A SENTENCE: THE PRONOUN I

Capitalize the first word of a sentence; capitalize the pronoun *I* whenever it appears in a sentence.

> Turn left at the corner.
> I never thought that I would see you again.
> If I leave, you can take my place.

TRY-OUT EXERCISE

Directions: Rekey the following sentences, capitalizing wherever necessary.

1. my neighbor is also my good friend.
2. please tell me why you think that i am wrong.
3. would you care to accompany me to the ballet?
4. on that test i received a high grade.
5. today i have an appointment after school.

1-2 PROPER NOUNS

A noun is a person, place, or thing. There are two kinds of nouns: common nouns and proper nouns. A common noun refers to members of a group of people or things. Common nouns are not capitalized. A proper noun refers to a *particular* person, place, or thing. Proper nouns are capitalized. Note the differences between the following common and proper nouns.

Common Nouns	Proper Nouns
girl	Nilda
boy	Harold
man	Mr. William Purdy
doctor	Dr. Laureen Langer
building	Empire State Building
canyon	Grand Canyon
day	Saturday
month	October
holiday	Easter
country	Great Britain
company	Walters & Company
corporation	Karig Corporation
committee	Finance Committee

A common noun such as *building* can refer to any building, and it is not capitalized; however, *building* is capitalized when it is part of the proper noun *Empire State Building*.

> A new high school is being built in our neighborhood. (*high school* is a common noun)

> My friends attend Thomas Jefferson High School. (*High School* is part of a proper noun)

> I live on a quiet street.
> I live on Baker Street.

> Janette is in the hospital.
> Janette is in St. Mary's Hospital.

> The ship will sail across the ocean.
> The ship will sail across the Pacific Ocean.

TRY-OUT EXERCISE

Directions: Rekey the following sentences, capitalizing nouns wherever necessary.

1. We flew to california during the christmas vacation.
2. Let's meet dan at the ford building on third avenue.
3. On monday, march 25, joe saw his doctor.
4. I learned that new york city is a major city in the united states.
5. My sister works in this building for a large company.

1-3 PERSONAL TITLES

Do not capitalize a person's title when it is not followed by the person's name.

> My uncle will be visiting us.
> The senator is running for reelection.
> Our chemistry professor is lecturing today.

Capitalize a person's title when it is used with the person's name as part of a proper noun.

> I'm happy that Uncle Andy will be visiting us.
> Her office announced that Senator Rand is running for reelection.
> Will you attend Professor Garcia's lecture today?

TRY-OUT EXERCISE

Directions: Rekey the following sentences, selecting the correct word in parentheses.

1. This gift is from (aunt, Aunt) Mathilda.
2. The (mayor, Mayor) and (governor, Governor) Ball are expected to attend.
3. My parents met with (dean, Dean) Cauldwell and the (principal, Principal).
4. Today (president, President) Harris asked me to act as (president, President) of the club during his absence.
5. Josh Hardy, our (doctor, Doctor), is on vacation.

1-4 TITLES OF BOOKS, MAGAZINES, AND NEWSPAPERS

Titles of books, magazines, and newspapers may be keyed in one of two ways:

1. IN ALL CAPITAL LETTERS
2. Underscored. Capitalize the first word and the important words of the title. Do not capitalize articles (a, an, the) or short prepositions and conjunctions (such as and, as, at, but, by, if, of, or, to, up) unless they are the first words in the title.

I read the book entitled AN AVENUE TO THE TOP OF THE WORLD.
I read the book entitled An Avenue to the Top of the World.

TRY-OUT EXERCISE

Directions: Rekey the following sentences, indicating the titles correctly.

1. Have you read the book entitled of mice and men?
2. My teacher assigned the book up the down staircase.
3. I must read a walk in a garden of roses.
4. Tess is the author of how to win friends and keep them.
5. Eating your way to fame and fortune is a very funny book.

1-5 SEASONS OF THE YEAR

Do not capitalize seasons of the year.

I look forward to every summer.
Jerry is shopping for winter clothing.
In the spring we seed the garden.

TRY-OUT EXERCISE

Directions: Rekey the following sentences, selecting the correct word in parentheses.

1. My grandmother visits us in the (spring, Spring), and we visit her during the (summer, Summer).
2. I enjoy going to football games in the (fall, Fall).
3. Patty will use her new sled this (winter, Winter).
4. In the (spring, Spring) our class will visit the zoo.
5. Last (summer, Summer) was hot, and the (fall, Fall) was damp.

1-6 PLACE NAMES AND GEOGRAPHICAL TERMS

Do not capitalize words such as north, south, east, west, northwestern, southwestern, etc., when they are used to tell a direction or location. Capitalize such words if they refer to regions of the country or of the world.

Walk south on Madison Street to reach the library.
BUT
The South is noted for its gracious hospitality.

Jimmy lives two miles southwest of Albany.
BUT
Jo is moving to the Southwest because of the climate.

The storm is visible at the eastern end of the horizon.
BUT
We import oil from the Middle East.

Directions: Rekey the following sentences, selecting the correct word or words in parentheses.

1. Those birds fly (south, South) every winter.
2. Years ago prospectors discovered gold in the (west, West).
3. Japan is located in the (far east, Far East).
4. The climate in the (northeast, Northeast) is cooler than the climate in the (southwestern, Southwestern) part of the country.
5. Keep driving (west, West) to reach Main Street.

1-7
SALUTATION AND COMPLIMENTARY CLOSE IN A LETTER

Capitalize the first word and all names and titles (Mr., Mrs., Miss, Ms., etc.) in a salutation. Capitalize the first word of the complimentary close.

Dear Carmen	Very truly yours
Dear Mrs. Laskey	Sincerely yours
Ladies and Gentlemen	Sincerely
Dear Mr. McCoy	Yours very truly
Dear Sir	Cordially yours

REVIEW OF PROOFREADER'S MARKS

Mark	Meaning	Example	Result
≣	All caps	Wuthering Heights	WUTHERING HEIGHTS
Cap or ≡	Capitalize	english	English
◡	Close up	can not	cannot
ℛ	Delete	I am not going.	I am going.
∧	Insert	Jay is ^{not} ill.	Jay is not ill.
⊙	Insert period	I came late I was lost.	I came late. I was lost.
# ∧	Insert space	It's not raining.	It's not raining.
lc or /	Lowercase letter	Friend	friend
⌐	Move left	Ned applied for a summer job.	Ned applied for a summer job.
⌐	Move right	The plane will leave shortly.	The plane will leave shortly.
¶	Paragraph	I had a nice time.¶I hope to see you very soon.	I had a nice time. I hope to see you very soon.
stet	Let it stand; ignore correction	We don't believe you.	We don't believe you.
∿	transpose	cheif	chief

SENTENCE EXERCISE

Directions: Rekey the following sentences in the spaces provided, capitalizing wherever necessary.

EXAMPLE:

if i hurry, i can meet uncle moe at the train.

If I hurry, I can meet Uncle Moe at the train.

1. the book entitled in the silence of the night was assigned by professor braun.

_____

2. on saturday we are moving to new york city, which is in the northeastern part of the country.

_____

_____

3. in class i learned that the civil war was fought between the north and the south.

_____

4. during easter aunt hanna was in mercy hospital; she became ill while visiting the middle east.

_____

_____

5. in the spring our doctor bought a house on atlantic street; it faces the ocean.

_____

6. did you know that my uncle is the president of moran corporation?

_____

7. the daily star reported that the prime minister of england will tour the southern states in october.

_____

_____

8. alex cooper's latest book, a history of the world in which we live, is this winter's best seller.

_____

_____

9. in july we will visit yellowstone national park; i am looking forward to seeing the park.

_____

_____

10. the governor will meet with judge willis to discuss reopening the city's hospital.

_____

DICTIONARY USAGE

Directions: Here are the more difficult words and their meanings that appear in the assignments in this unit. Study them carefully; complete the sentences that follow.

annex (noun)	an additional building
benefit (verb)	to help, provide aid
campaign (noun)	the process of running for public office
commendation	praise
committee	a group of persons appointed for certain duties
flier	a circular, a notice
landmark	a building of unusual historical interest
publicity	information issued to gain public attention or support
sponsor (verb)	to pay the expenses of an undertaking
volunteer (verb)	to offer himself/herself for a service or duty

Directions for completing the following sentences: Select the appropriate word from the above list, and key it in each blank.

1. A _____ announcing the store-wide sale was mailed to each customer.
2. The bank will _____ the annual bicycle race; it will provide the prizes.
3. Tess received a letter of _____ from her employer for her fine work.
4. A member of the House of Representatives must conduct a _____ for reelection every two years.
5. Buckingham Palace is a _____ in London.
6. The proceeds of the Women's Club luncheon will _____ the local orphanage.
7. The movie had received much advance _____, and the theater was crowded.
8. My classroom is not in the main building; it is in the _____.
9. My father, who is an accountant, will _____ as a fireman in his spare time.
10. A _____ was appointed to investigate the accident.

Directions: Key this personal note in block style with open punctuation. It contains 34 words that should be capitalized.

Use a full sheet of paper.
Margins: 60-space line (elite 21-86; pica 12-77)

All parts of the note are to be keyed at the left margin. Key the date on the 15th line from the top edge of the paper. Quadruple-space, and key the salutation. Double-space after the salutation, and single-space the body. Double-space after the body; key the complimentary close.

---

february 3, 19--

dear sue

every spring the barkley company sponsors a dance on memorial
day to benefit a special charity, and students of whitman
high school lend assistance. last year our school helped
raise money for the rock ledge animal shelter. this year's
monies will go to sacred heart hospital's new annex at the
northern end of town.

our principal, mr. sims, sends letters of commendation to
students who volunteer to help; and the president of the
barkley company presents them with silver pins.

sue, i am on the committee handling publicity for the dance.
we place ads in the local paper, news daily, and distribute
fliers. we invite you to join us on the publicity committee.

sincerely

Directions: Key this personal note in modified block style with indented paragraphs and open punctuation. Capitalize wherever necessary.

Use a full sheet of paper.
Margins: 50-space line (elite 26-81; pica 17-72)
Tabs: Elite 31, 51; pica 22,42
Center point: Elite 51; pica 42

Key the date at the center of the 15th line from the top edge of the paper. Quadruple-space, and key the salutation. Double-space after the salutation, and single-space the body. Double-space after the body; key the complimentary close at the center point of the paper.

---

september 25, 19--

dear harry

¶ my uncle, ted smithers, is senator coulter's campaign manager. last summer my parents allowed me to spend four weeks traveling with uncle ted and the senator.

¶ most of our time was spent in the south. in each city we met the mayor; in atlanta, georgia, we even met the governor. the senator spoke at fund-raising dinners and on college campuses.

¶ when i left, the senator and his wife margie presented me with goodbye gifts. he gave me a ring from the far east; and margie gave me a subscription to my favorite magazine, a typical teen.

¶ i hope to see you during the christmas recess.

sincerely

Directions: Key the following short report, capitalizing wherever necessary.

Use a full sheet of paper.
Margins: 60-space line (elite 21-86; pica 12-77)
Tabs: Elite 26, pica 17
Center points: Elite 51; pica 42

Center the title (KEY IN ALL CAPITAL LETTERS) on the 12th line from the top edge of the paper for elite and the 10th line for pica. Quadruple-space to the first paragraph. Double-space the report. Indent paragraphs 5 spaces.

```
                        my trip to italy


     this past summer was very enjoyable.  in july i visited
italy with my parents, my brother ed, and aunt edna.

     my favorite landmark was the leaning tower of pisa.
although i had read about it in my studies at william tell
high school, seeing the tower for the first time was a thrill.

     we spent three weeks sightseeing in major cities and then
relaxed near lake como, which is in the northern part of italy.
i practiced speaking italian (i am studying it in high school)
and was very successful.

     our last stop was rome.  my aunt has friends there, and
they showed us around the city.

     we flew home to chicago with a lot of wonderful memories.
```

CONTEXT CHECK

(What is the
communication about?)

Directions: Following are three groups of sentences concerning the two letters and the report in this unit that you have keyed. Fill in the blanks; you may refer to the communications.

HELPFUL-HINT LETTER

1. Last year the writer helped raise money for the _____.
2. The principal expresses appreciation to students who volunteer to help by sending them _____.
3. Of which committee is the writer a member? _____

YOU'RE ON YOUR OWN—ASSIGNMENT NO. 1

1. The writer's uncle is Senator Coulter's _____.
2. As a goodbye gift from the senator, the writer received a _____ _____.
3. While the writer was with the senator, in what part of the country did they spend most of their time? _____

YOU'RE ON YOUR OWN—ASSIGNMENT NO. 2

1. The author's favorite landmark was _____.
2. After three weeks of sightseeing, the author and his/her family relaxed near _____.
3. The last stop before flying home was _____.

PROOFREADING ASSIGNMENT

Directions: Insert proofreader's marks to indicate corrections in the following paragraph. Here are the 6 marks that will have to be inserted.

≡	capitalize	the lock is broken.	The lock is broken.
⸋	delete	I likes turkey.	I like turkey.
∧	insert	He's a rich man.	He's a rich man.
#	insert space	Come with me.	Come with me.
/	lowercase letter	Drink the Milk.	Drink the milk.
⌐	move left	Don't be late. I won't wait.	Don't be late. I won't wait.

My aunt's house is haunted. Doors closse by themselves, floors

creak when noone is walking, and there are strange noses during

the night. Last friday at Midnight all the lights in the house

went on by themselves.

2 Subject and Verb Agreement

Performance Objective:

Upon completion of this unit, you will be able to apply rules for subject and verb agreement in written communications.

Every sentence has at least one subject and at least one verb. The subject is the person, place, or thing that the sentence is about. The verb expresses the action of the subject. In the following examples, the subject(s) is underscored one time; the verb(s) is underscored twice.

The boy caught the ball.
Roberto passed the test.
Beulah and Freddie watched the baseball game.
I laughed and cried during the movie.
Listen to my instructions. (NOTE: This is an imperative sentence or command; the subject is the implied *you*.)

2-1 SINGULAR AND PLURAL SUBJECTS

The subject and verb of a sentence must agree.

If the subject is singular, the verb is singular.
The girl is angry.

If the subject is plural, the verb is plural.
The girls are angry.

If there is more than one subject, the verb is plural.
The girl and her mother are angry.

TRY-OUT EXERCISE

Directions: Rekey the following sentences, choosing the correct verb in parentheses.

1. The clowns (is, are) traveling with the circus.
2. Our cat (likes, like) to curl up on the sofa.
3. The stove and refrigerator (was, were) repaired.
4. Today the bacon and eggs (tastes, taste) better.
5. My father (walks, walk) to work every day.

2-2 VERBS SEPARATED FROM SUBJECTS

Sometimes a verb does not immediately follow the subject. Don't be misled. The verb must still agree with the subject of the sentence.

These <u>flowers</u> in the light blue vase <u>are</u> no longer fresh.
The <u>puppet</u> on the strings <u>dances</u> to the lively tune.
That <u>man</u> with the two suitcases <u>looks</u> like my uncle.

TRY-OUT EXERCISE

Directions: Rekey the following sentences, choosing the correct verb in parentheses.

1. Ten desks in my cousin Judy's classroom (have, has) been painted.
2. That pretty girl with the blue eyes (is, are) my best friend.
3. Students in the cooking class (bake, bakes) on Friday.
4. The car with the dented fenders (belongs, belong) to my cousin.
5. The man who is with the four women (look, looks) angry.

2-3 EITHER-OR; NEITHER-NOR

When two singular subjects are joined by *or* or *nor*, the verb is singular.

Either Ronnie or Vicky represents the class at meetings.
Either winter or fall is a nice time of year.
Neither the colonel nor the private was in uniform today.

When two plural verbs are joined by *or* or *nor*, use a plural verb.

Either freshmen or seniors are selected for those jobs.
Either red pencils or blue pencils have to be used.
Neither the buses nor the trains were on time today.

When a singular subject and a plural subject are joined by *or* or *nor*, the verb agrees with the subject that is closer to it.

Neither the dog nor the cats are wearing licenses.
Either my parents or my sister intends to buy me a bicycle.
Neither the teacher nor her students were at the assembly.

TRY-OUT EXERCISE

Directions: Rekey the following sentences, choosing the correct verb in parentheses.

1. Either the editor or the faculty adviser (approves, approve) yearbook articles.
2. Neither Rachel nor her classmates (is, are) pleased about the test.
3. Neither the mechanics nor their supervisor (plans, plan) to repair the car.
4. Either her friends or her sisters (intends, intend) to give Marcie a bridal shower.
5. Neither Mr. Goldman nor his son (has, have) seen Muriel.

2-4 SPECIAL SINGULAR CASES

Use a singular verb when one of the following words is the subject of a sentence:

anybody	everybody	one
anyone	everyone	somebody
each	nobody	someone

Everybody believes it is the truth.
Nobody knows the trouble I've seen.
Anyone answering the door receives a sample.

TRY-OUT EXERCISE

Directions: Rekey the following sentences, choosing the correct word in parentheses.

1. Each of the tenants (want, wants) to install an alarm.
2. Not everyone (agrees, agree) with the speaker.
3. If nobody (claim, claims) the treasure, you may keep it.
4. I hope that someone (are, is) coming to my aid.
5. Everybody (knows, know) the truth about him.

SENTENCE EXERCISE

Directions: Rekey the following sentences in the spaces provided, choosing the correct verb in parentheses.

EXAMPLE

My feet (is, are) wet from walking in the rain.

My feet are wet from walking in the rain.

1. This morning I (feel, feels) lazy.

_____

2. The airplane to New York and Boston (is, are) leaving on time.

_____

3. The president and his assistants (appears, appear) at every meeting.

_____

4. Either Dr. Smith or his nurse (is, are) available.

_____

5. Everybody in his two classes (likes, like) Mr. Foster.

_____

6. Arlene and Marlene (was, were) best friends.

_____

7. Neither the bulls nor the cows (is, are) in the barn.

_____

8. Each of the five clerks (takes, take) a coffee break.

_____

9. The red-haired girl with the dimples (is, are) my father's secretary.

_____

10. Either Charlotte or her sisters (intends, intend) to go to the prom.

_____

DICTIONARY USAGE

Directions: Here are the more difficult words and their meanings that appear in the assignments in this unit. Study them carefully; complete the sentences that follow.

bridal shower	a party in honor of an engaged girl at which presents are given to her
consider	to think about
express (verb)	to make known one's opinion
faculty (of a school)	teachers
fiancé	a man to whom a girl is engaged
grapevine	an informal means of airing information or gossip
issue (of a magazine)	the total quantity of a publication printed at one time
newsworthy	interesting enough to report
pool (verb)	to put money into one common fund for a special purpose
preference	the favoring of one thing over another

Directions for completing the following sentences: Select the appropriate word from the above list, and key it in each blank.

1. Ginny's _____ gave her a beautiful engagement ring.
2. In your order, please state your color _____ .
3. I hear through the _____ that your brother is getting married.
4. If we _____ our money, we can buy Maggie a more expensive gift.
5. Thank you for your suggestion; I will _____ it.
6. My sister is engaged; at her _____ she received five toasters.
7. Our editor told us to report only _____ items.
8. The _____ of our school is small; only 20 are on staff.
9. Felix purchased the special anniversary _____ of that magazine.
10. I want to _____ my thanks for all the gifts that I received at my _____ .

Directions: Key this personal note in block style with open punctuation. It contains 7 instances in which the verb does not agree with its subject(s), which you are to correct.

Use a full sheet of paper.
Margins: 50-space line (elite 26-81; pica 17-72)

All parts of the note are to be keyed at the left margin. Key the date on the 15th line from the top edge of the paper. Quadruple-space, and key the salutation. Double-space after the salutation, and single-space the body. Double-space after the body; key the complimentary close.

November 5, 19--

Dear Luis

I can't meet you this week because I am going to the football game with Chuck and Randy. The boys and I was able to buy the tickets because we worked every Saturday last year.

The game is the last one of the season, and nobody want to miss it.

Chuck's two older brothers, Carl and Marty, is also going. Neither Carl nor Marty live in town; they drives here just for the games. Since Saturday is my birthday, the boys is taking me to lunch before the game.

Let me know which weekend during the next three weeks look like a good time for us to meet.

Sincerely

Directions: Key this personal note in modified block style with indented paragraphs and open punctuation. Correct any verbs that do not agree with their subjects.

Use a full sheet of paper.
Margins: 60-space line (elite 21-86; pice 12-77)
Tabs: Elite 26, 51; pica 17, 42
Center points: Elite 51; pice 42

Key the date at the center of the 15th line from the top edge of the paper. Quadruple-space, and key the salutation. Double-space after the salutation, and single-space the body. Double-space after the body; key the complimentary close at the center point of the paper.

March 7, 19--

Dear FloraDalis

Aunt Cora, one of my favorite aunts, plan to be married in May. Two of her closest friends, Donna and Maris, is giving her a bridal shower in April.

I can't decide what to give Aunt Cora. She and her future husband is moving into a new house after the wedding, and everyone know that they can use many things. Neither Aunt Cora nor her fiancé have expressed any preferences.

My two sisters and I am considering giving Aunt Cora one gift from the three of us. If we pools our money, we could buy a more expensive gift.

FloraDalis, what do you think? You has good taste. Can you suggest a gift for Aunt Cora's shower?

Sincerely

Directions: Key the following short report, correcting any verbs that do not agree with their subjects. Refer to page 5 for a review of proofreader's marks.

Use a full sheet of paper.
Margins: 60-space line (elite 21-86; pica 12-77)
Tabs: Elite 26; pica 17
Center points: Elite 51; pica 42

Key the title on line 12 from the top of the paper for elite and line 10 for pica. Double-space the report. Indent paragraphs 5 spaces.

NOTE: You will not be able to copy this report line for line. Use your judgment as to where each line should end within the margins given.

Center *quadruple space*

The Grapevine

When the students decided to have a school news paper, Mr. Winters, one of our english teachers, were helpful in telling us how to begin. The Editor was carefully chosen, *and reporters* Mr. Winters was asked to become faculty *and* adviser. A contest was held to find a name for the newspaper, and the grapevine was born. ¶ Everyone were invited to contribute by giving to the reporters any newsworthy *stet* items. The first issue was about the school picnic. ¶ Our newspaper, needless to say, were a sucess. Neither the students nor the teachers is able to understand how we lived without it. Every body look forward to recieving each issue of THE GRAPEVINE.

CONTEXT CHECK

[What is the communication about?]

Directions: Following are 3 groups of sentences concerning the 2 letters and the report in this unit that you have keyed. Fill in the blanks; you may refer to the communications.

HELPFUL-HINT LETTER

1. The writer and his/her friends were able to buy tickets to the game because _____.
2. No one wants to miss this game because _____.
3. When is the writer's birthday? _____

YOU'RE ON YOUR OWN—ASSIGNMENT NO. 1

1. In April two of Aunt Cora's friends are giving her a _____.
2. Has Aunt Cora or her fiancé expressed any gift preferences? (Fill in "yes" or "no.") _____
3. The writer and his/her two sisters are considering _____ their money and buying one expensive gift.

YOU'RE ON YOUR OWN—ASSIGNMENT NO. 2

1. The name of the school newspaper is _____.
2. Mr. Winters is the _____ of the school newspaper.
3. The first issue of the newspaper was about the _____.

PROOFREADING ASSIGNMENT

Directions: Insert proofreader's marks to indicate corrections in the following paragraph. Here are the 6 marks that will have to be inserted.

⌒	close up	every one	everyone
ℒ	delete	I'm ~~very~~ sorry.	I'm sorry.
∧	insert	The room is qiet.	The room is quiet.
⊙	insert period	Let's goIt's late.	Let's go. It's late.
⌐	move right	___I find it difficult to understand.	I find it difficult to understand.
∿	transpose	beleive	believe

Today is a lovely sp ring day. You can hear hear the birds in

the trees The sky is blue, and there are soft whte clouds

floating in the sky. The breeze is as soft as a whisper;

summer is in teh air.

3 Personal Pronouns

Performance Objective:

Upon completion of this unit, you will be able to apply rules for proper usage of personal pronouns in written communications.

We have already learned that a noun is a person, place, or thing. A personal pronoun takes the place of a noun.

In the following sentences, note how a personal pronoun can be substituted for a noun.

<u>Constance</u> is only five feet tall.	(Noun: Constance)
<u>She</u> is only five feet tall.	(Pronoun: She)
The <u>glass</u> is empty.	(Noun: glass)
<u>It</u> is empty.	(Pronoun: It)
<u>Dr. Morgan</u> lives far from his <u>brother</u>.	(Nouns: Dr. Morgan brother)
<u>He</u> lives far from <u>him</u>.	(Pronouns: He, him)

The words listed below are personal pronouns:

	Singular	Plural
Group A	I	we
	you	you
	he, she, it	they
Group B	me	us
	you	you
	him, her, it	them

3-1
PERSONAL PRONOUNS: TWO SUBJECTS JOINED BY *AND*

The subject is the person, place, or thing that the sentence or clause is about. When two or more subjects are joined by *and*, use the pronouns from Group A of the pronoun list.

Jack and <u>she</u> went up the hill.
<u>He</u> and <u>I</u> joined the choir.
Benny and <u>we</u> will be on time.

TRY-OUT EXERCISE

Directions: Rekey the following sentences, choosing the correct pronoun in parentheses.

1. My friend and (me, I) are learning to play the piano.
2. (Her, She) and (we, us) skated this morning.
3. Ralph and (they, them) were at the game.
4. (Us, We) and Joanna are first cousins.
5. For Halloween, (he, him) and (me, I) bought pumpkins.

3-2 PERSONAL PRONOUN AFTER THE VERB *TO BE*

The verb expresses the action of the subject. When one or more personal pronouns follow the verb *to be* (am, are, is, was, were), use the pronouns from Group A of the pronoun list.

It is I.
The culprits were they.
The winners are she and he.

TRY-OUT EXERCISE

Directions: Rekey the following sentences, choosing the correct pronoun in parentheses.

1. The honored guests were (she, her) and the mayor.
2. I think it was (them, they) who broke the window.
3. Is it (we, us) who must vote today?
4. Can it be (he, him)? No, it is (me, I).
5. The owners of the dog are Sonny and (her, she).

3-3 PERSONAL PRONOUN AFTER A PREPOSITION

A preposition is a connecting word such as the following:

at	for	to
before	from	with
between	of	without
by	on	

When one or more personal pronouns follow a preposition, use the pronouns from Group B of the pronoun list.

He received the book from us.
Jim sat between him and me.
We arrived before them and her.

TRY-OUT EXERCISE

Directions: Rekey the following sentences, choosing the correct pronoun in parentheses.

1. Tammie gave the papers to Rhoda and (he, him).
2. The accident was witnessed by (they, them) and (us, we).
3. The Christmas gifts were for (her, she) and (I, me).
4. At the movies Miguel sat between Sam and (we, us).
5. I don't see the twins; we will leave without (them, they).

SENTENCE EXERCISE

Directions: Rekey the following sentences in the spaces provided, choosing the correct pronoun in parentheses.

EXAMPLE:

I told the truth to (he, him) and (she, her).
I told the truth to him and her.

1. His father and (he, him) tarred the leaky roof.

_____

2. It was (them, they) who broke the window in the garage.

_____

3. Ann and (him, he) brought home three stray cats.

_____

4. Jerry spilled the milk on Fanny and (I, me).

_____

5. The bus passed by (us, we) and (they, them) without stopping.

_____

6. Marc and (me, I) will decorate the tree for Christmas.

_____

7. I think that it is (her, she) who should be elected class president.

_____

8. If they do not arrive soon, the meeting will begin without (he, him) and (her, she).

_____

9. The villains in the story were (he, him) and the old woman.

_____

10. (We, Us) and (them, they) were absent today because of the snow.

_____

DICTIONARY USAGE

Directions: Here are the more difficult words and their meanings that appear in the assignments in this unit. Study them carefully; complete the sentences that follow.

dude ranch	a vacation resort offering horseback riding
encourage	to give confidence to; urge
enroll	to enter or register on a list
inseparable	always together
intrigue (noun)	secret scheme or plot
major (adjective)	greater in importance, size, or amount
Orient (noun)	countries or territories in East Asia; for example, China, Japan, Hong Kong
reluctant	unwilling

Directions for completing the following sentences: Select the appropriate word from the above list, and key it in each blank.

1. The two friends are _____; they go everywhere together.
2. As a remembrance of his trip to the _____, my uncle brought me pearls from Japan.
3. A _____ portion of the school budget goes for books.
4. Kathleen went to a _____ over the weekend and learned to ride a horse.
5. My parents tried to _____ me to study so that I could pass the test.
6. I am _____ to walk the dog because he always runs away from me.
7. Cappie will _____ in a French course over the summer.
8. I love to read stories of _____ and adventure.
9. China is a _____ country in the _____.
10. Her mother tried to _____ Martha to learn to ice skate, but Martha was _____ to do so because she was afraid of falling.

Directions: Key this personal note in modified block style with open punctuation. It contains 7 instances in which a personal pronoun is not used properly. Make the necessary corrections.

Use a full sheet of paper.
Margins: 50-space line (elite 26-81; pica 17-72)
Tabs and center points: Elite 51; pica 42

Key the date at the center of the 15th line from the top edge of the paper. Quadruple-space, and key the salutation. Double-space after the salutation, and single-space the body. Double-space after the body; key the complimentary close at the center point of the paper.

October 17, 19--

Dear Uncle Otto

¶ My friend Claire and me went to a dude ranch with our families over the weekend, and we rode horses.

¶ Between you and I, we had the best time of our lives. We had worried that our parents might be reluctant to let us ride; in fact, it was them who encouraged us to ride every day.

¶ Claire and I made two new friends, Lilly and Billy. Them and we became inseparable. Lilly and Billy are cousins. Her and he live in California; they have already sent invitations to Claire and I to visit them.

¶ Uncle Otto, I am anxious to show you pictures of my friends and I on horseback.

Sincerely

Directions: Key this personal-business letter in block style with open punctuation. Correct any personal pronouns that are not used properly.

Use a full sheet of paper.
Margins: 50-space line (elite 26-81; pica 17-72)

All parts of the letter are to be keyed at the left margin. Key your return address on the 13th line from the top edge of the paper; the date is on line 15 under your two-line return address. Quadruple-space after the date, and key the inside address (name and address of person to whom the letter is going). Double-space; key the salutation. Double-space after the salutation, and single-space the body. Double-space after the body; key the complimentary close. Quadruple-space, and key your name.

Your street address
Your city, state ZIP
December 1, 19--

Mr. Angelo Lopez
Office Manager
Warden & Company
300 Baron Street
Savannah, GA 31401-1603

Dear Mr. Lopez

My cousin, Bill Morgan, and me are enrolled in a
computer class in our school. Him and I enjoy it
very much. Several of our classmates and us have
decided to work in that field one day.

It was me who suggested to the class that we arrange
to visit major computer centers. Each pair of students will visit a different one; our teacher,
Ms. Flor, suggested to Bill and I that we contact
you. Her and we hope that a visit to your company
can be arranged.

Seeing your computer center would be a great experience for Bill and I.

Cordially

Your name

Directions: Key the following short report, correcting any personal pronouns that are not used properly.

Use a full sheet of paper.
Margins: 60-space line (elite 21-86; pica 12-77)
Tabs: Elite 26, pica 17
Center points: Elite 51; pica 42

Center the title (KEY IN ALL CAPITAL LETTERS) on line 12 from the top edge of the paper for elite and line 10 for pica. Quadruple-space to the first paragraph. Double-space the report. Indent paragraphs 5 spaces.

A TRIP TO TOWN

My name is Mandy. I have three sisters: Mary, Missy, and Maudy. Maudy and me attend the same school. Mary is the oldest; her and Missy go to another school.

One day Mary suggested to Missy, Maudy, and I that we meet in town after school to see a movie about intrigue in the Orient. We all thought it was a good idea. Unfortunately, Mary and Missy missed their bus; and them and we did not meet on time. Maudy and me wondered what had happened; she and me waited an hour. When they finally arrived, it was too late to see the movie. It was me who had the idea of stopping for pizza and going home.

I told Mary that the next time I go to a movie after school, it will be without she and Missy.

CONTEXT CHECK

[What is the
communication about?]

Directions: Following are three groups of sentences concerning the 2 letters and the report in this unit that you have keyed. Fill in the blanks; you may refer to the communications.

HELPFUL-HINT LETTER

1. Claire and the writer spent the weekend at a _____.
2. The names of their two new friends are _____ and _____ .
3. Their two new friends live in _____ .

YOU'RE ON YOUR OWN—ASSIGNMENT NO. 1

1. The two cousins are enrolled in _____ .
2. The writer suggested that the students visit _____ .
3. Each pair of students in the class will visit a _____ computer center.

YOU'RE ON YOUR OWN—ASSIGNMENT NO. 2

1. The names of the four sisters are _____ , _____ , _____ and _____ .
2. The girls wanted to see a movie about _____ .
3. The girls didn't see the movie because _____ .

PROOFREADING ASSIGNMENT

Directions: Insert proofreader's marks to indicate corrections in the following paragraph. Here are the 6 marks that will have to be inserted.

☰	capitalize	Is jay present?	Is Jay present?
⊃	close up	hap py	happy
⌿	delete (take out)	abssent	absent
∧	insert	Jay is thre.	Jay is there.
/	lowercase letter	Is Jay There?	Is Jay there?
∾	transpose	centre	center

my friend Jilly and and I went to a rock concert over the

week end. It took place in a large thaeter near our

Home. Aftr the show we bought the group's latest record.

Review Lesson Units 1-3

NAME _____

SENTENCE REVIEW

Directions: Rekey the following sentences in the spaces provided, capitalizing wherever necessary; make any necessary corrections in subject and verb agreement and in pronoun usage.

EXAMPLE:

my uncle who has four dogs and two cats are visiting us.

My uncle who has four dogs and two cats is visiting us.

1. the governor won reelection in november.

_____

2. this term zeke and me have jobs after school.

_____

3. neither clara nor her two sisters was able to be here.

_____

4. everyone in the history classes have been notified of the test date.

_____

5. this past winter we went skiing in the northeastern part of the country.

_____

6. was it her or he who had the flu?

_____

7. the lady with the heavy packages are waiting for a taxi.

_____

8. my aunt want to give me the book entitled the world is a stage.

_____

9. us and she gave celeste a surprise party.

_____

10. between you and i, visiting florida was the most fun.

_____

11. why don't somebody answer the bell?

_____

12. tom and his handsome younger brother is on the soccer team.

_____

13. do you know if uncle bobbie like the gift from paula and i?

_____

14. either my brother or father water the lawn during the summer.

_____

15. it was me who accidentally broke the window.

_____

Directions: Key this personal note in modified block style with open punctuation. Use a full sheet of paper with a 60-space line. Capitalize wherever necessary; make any necessary corrections in subject and verb agreement and in pronoun usage.

september 8, 19--

dear aunt emma

this past summer, after reading the magazine entitled camping life, i went on an overnight camping trip with my two friends, millie and claudette.

we hiked along the trails of the lovely wooded park at the northern end of town. we stopped to eat the lunch that millie and me had packed. unfortunately, a blister soon developed on millie's foot; she walked between claudette and i for support. neither millie nor claudette were sorry when we stopped and set up camp.

that evening my two friends and me sat around the fire telling ghost stories. the next morning it was me who prepared breakfast; then we was on our way home after a most enjoyable experience.

everybody hope you will visit us soon, aunt emma.

sincerely

Directions: Key this personal note in block style with open punctuation. Use a full sheet of paper with a 60-space line. Capitalize wherever necessary; make any necessary corrections in subject and verb agreement and in pronoun usage.

january 5, 19--

dear janie

our annual winter student-faculty talent show took place just before christmas. everyone in town always look forward to it; even the mayor attends.

the teachers and us had a great time; mr. magner, our princi-pal, played the guitar; in fact, it was him who composed the show's music. him and the assistant principal then sang a duet. even dean benini performed; he have a rich tenor voice.

between you and i, janie, the best of the ten acts were the one in which ms. ames, my math teacher, performed magic tricks. i'll tell you more when i sees you next month.

either my mother or father are sure to meet you at the airport.

sincerely

PROOFREADING REVIEW

Directions: Insert proofreader's marks to indicate corrections in the following paragraph. Here are the 6 marks that will have to be inserted.

mark	meaning	before	after
≡	capitalize	it's foggy.	It's foggy.
⌒	close up	will ingly	willingly
℣	delete	overwhelm	overwhelm
∧	insert	overwelm	overwhelm
⊙	insert period	I can't see	I can't see.
∿	transpose	cheif	chief

As everyone knows, magic is an ilusion. Yet we sometimes see faets performed that makes us wonder for example, have you ever seen someone sawed in half, or rise in the air with out any support, or simply disappear?

4 Homonyms

Upon completion of this unit, you will be able to differentiate between
words that sound alike but have different meanings.

Homonyms are two or more words that sound alike but have different
meanings.

The weather is fair.   The postman delivered the mail.
I don't know whether to go.   My dog Scottie is a male.

Here are additional examples of frequently used sound-alike words.

An ant is crawling on the stem.   Have you heard the news?
My aunt has red hair.   The farmer has a herd of cows.

The shelf is bare of food.   Our cat dug a hole.
Let's visit the bear in the zoo.   I ate the whole pizza.

He blew his auto horn.   The trip takes one hour.
Lottie wore a blue dress.   Our neighbor is friendly.

Did you buy the fruit?   We don't know where to look.
I am going by your house.   There are no tickets left.

Jenny is a dear friend.   The bullet is made of lead.
The hunter saw the deer.   The scout led the way.

He hurt his eye.   My desk is made of wood.
I am not well.   The maid answered the door.

Pay the fare on the train.   This meat is not cooked.
The judge tried to be fair.   Can you meet me?

I flew in an airplane.   The miner dug the coal.
Jerry has the flu.   A child is a minor.

This recipe requires flour.   One person is unable to come.
Callie picked a red flower.   She won first prize.

Max was ill for two days.   I bought a pair of shoes.
She has four sisters.   Pare the skin of the orange.
                                   Willy ate the pear.
Please grate the onion.
A great many people are here.   Hurray, I passed the test.
                                   We moved this past winter.
We heard her groan with pain.
You have grown so tall.   We wish for peace on earth.
                                   Danny ate a piece of pie.
They guessed the truth.
Be our guest this weekend.

Can you hear me?
Here is Matthew.

The mistake is plain to see.
The plane arrived on time.

The school principals met today.
We ordered the book PRINCI-
  PLES OF ELECTRICITY.

Have you read that book?
My favorite color is red.

You're right; I'm wrong.
Write Jake a letter.

We crossed the road with care.
I rode a horse last weekend.

The ship will sail at noon.
That store is having a sale.

The sea is rough today.
I see her in the distance.

Let's buy some fruit.
I owe the sum of $10.

I was taught never to steal.
The table is made of steel.

I heard the bells peal.
Please peel the apple.

Don't step on the dog's tail.
Katie read the fairy tale.

The girls heard their mother.
Who is standing there?

The pitcher threw the ball.
I walked through the door.

Sylvia is flying to Spain.
We, too, are going there.
Carry the two suitcases.

They would not wait for me.
Have you lost weight?

We lost our way.
I weigh 100 pounds.

The virus made me feel weak.
I'll see you in a week.

Which one should I buy?
The witch sat on her broomstick.

The chair is made of wood.
I would not answer.

**TRY-OUT
EXERCISE**

Directions: Rekey the following sentences, selecting the correct word in parentheses.

1. I will (mail, male) the letter telling Melissa that we will (meat, meet) her soon.
2. Jilly has (groan, grown) (to, too, two) inches since last year.
3. The child (lead, led) the (way, weigh) to the lake.
4. I think that the desk of (steal, steel) is heavier than the desk that is (made, maid) of (wood, would).
5. After the (grate, great) war (their, there) was (peace, piece) for (one, won) year.

SENTENCE EXERCISE

Directions: Rekey the following sentences in the spaces provided, selecting the correct word in parentheses.

EXAMPLE:

I (heard, herd) that you were not well this (passed, past) winter.

I heard that you were not well this past winter.

1. We (one, won) a (pair, pare, pear) of tickets to the football game.

_____

2. Do you (know, no) at what time the bells will (peal, peel)?

_____

3. The (weather, whether) was not (fair, fare) today; the wind (blew, blue) as the rain fell.

_____

_____

4. This (passed, past) (weak, week) I learned that I (passed, past) the test.

_____

_____

5. Our (guessed, guest) brought my mother a single (flour, flower)—a (read, red) rose.

_____

6. I must (mail, male) a get-well card to my (ant, aunt); she has the (flew, flu) and has lost (wait, weight).

_____

_____

7. Do you (know, no) (weather, whether) Jack (wood, would) like a shirt for his birthday?

_____

_____

8. Please (buy, by) (to, too, two) onions to (grate, great) into the stew.

_____

9. We all loved the (tail, tale) about the prince and the (which, witch); even the dog wagged its (tail, tale).

_____

_____

10. I (heard, herd) that (their, there) was an accident on the (road, rode) this morning that tied up traffic for an (hour, our).

_____

_____

DICTIONARY USAGE

Directions: Here are the more difficult words and their meanings that appear in the assignments in this unit. Study them carefully; complete the sentences that follow.

alumni (plural of alumnus)	a graduate of a school
candidate	one who seeks an office or position
dedicate (verb)	to do something in honor of someone
hear (in a legal sense)	to listen to legal arguments in a court
nominate	to choose as a candidate for appointment or election
principles	accepted code of conduct
qualifications	the necessary skills that fit a person for certain work
unbiased	without prejudice; not leaning toward one opinion as opposed to another
weigh (verb) (to _____ facts)	to consider carefully
white elephant (_____ sale)	something not wanted by its owner that has value to others

Directions for completing the following sentences: Select the appropriate word from the above list, and key it in each blank.

1. The government official is known for his high _____; he works for the benefit of all citizens.
2. My brother is seeking a position as a computer operator; he has all the _____.
3. Our teacher will _____ carefully any question we ask him before he replies.
4. Our school is so proud; one of our _____ from the class of 1965 was just promoted to the presidency of his company.
5. Ken bought a pair of brass candlesticks at a _____ sale.
6. The umpire is known to be fair and _____ in making his decisions.
7. In 1980 Ronald Reagan was _____ by the Republican Party as its presidential _____.
8. The judge will _____ the case today, and I know that she will carefully _____ all the facts before making her decision.
9. The rich man donated the money to build the hospital, which he _____ to the memory of his late wife.
10. I cannot tell a lie; it is against my _____ to do so.

Directions: Key this personal note in block style with open punctuation. Correct the 16 homonyms that are not used properly.

Use a full sheet of paper.
Margins: 50-space line (elite 26-81; pica 17-72)

All parts of the note are to be keyed at the left margin. Key the date on the 15th line from the top edge of the paper. Quadruple-space, and key the salutation. Double-space after the salutation, and single-space the body. Double-space after the body; key the complimentary close.

January 5, 19--

Deer Celia

I have the flew this weak and will not be able to
help you at the annual white elephant sail.

My family has given me too baskets of items to sell:
a pare of bookends from my ant, some books of fairy
tails from my youngest brother, and a read dress
with a silk flour pin from my mother.

Unfortunately, eye can't deliver these. You might
have herd my grown when the doctor told me not to
leave the house four a week. Therefore, I wood
appreciate it if you could stop buy and pick up the
baskets.

Sincerely

Directions: Key this personal-business letter in modified block style with indented paragraphs and mixed punctuation. Correct any homonyms that are not used properly.

Use a full sheet of paper.
Margins: 50-space line (elite 26-81; pica 17-72)
Tabs: Elite 31, 51; pica 22, 42
Center points: Elite 51; pica 42

Key your return address at the center of the 13th line from the top edge of the paper; the date is on line 15 under your two-line return address. Quadruple-space after the date, and key the inside address (name and address of person to whom the letter is going). Double-space; key the salutation. Double-space after the salutation, and single-space the body. Double-space after the body; key the complimentary close at the center point. Quadruple-space, and key your name at the center point.

```
                                        Your street address
                                        Your city, state  ZIP
                                        September 16, 19--



        Mr. Peter Lulgjuraj
        Vice President
        Moorehead & Moorehead, Inc.
        433 Caldor Avenue
        Miami, FL  33140-8761

        Deer Mr. Lulgjuraj:

            On October 15 our new computer room will be
        dedicated to Arthur Jason, who was our principle
        four 30 years before retiring this passed year.

            The Business Club is inviting several alumni
        to be guessed speakers at the ceremony, at witch the
        hole department will be present.  Wood you care to
        be won of them?  The topic is "Careers in Business."

            We no the rode to success is rocky, but per-
        haps a peace of advice from each of our speakers
        could help us threw sum of the rockier moments.

            We hope that you can be here.  Their will be
        refreshments served.

                                        Sincerely,



                                        Your name
                                        President, Business Club
```

Directions: Key the following short report, correcting any homonyms that are not used properly. Refer to page 5 for a review of proofreader's marks.

Use a full sheet of paper.
Margins: 60-space line (elite 21-86; pica 12-77)
Tabs: Elite 26, pica 17
Center points: Elite 51, pica 42

Center the title on line 12 from the top edge of the paper for elite and line 10 for pica. Quadruple-space to the first paragraph. Double-space the report. Indent paragraphs 5 spaces.

NOTE: You will not be able to copy this report line for line. Use your judgment as to where each line should end within the margins given.

Center ☐ The Supreme Court *)quadruple space*

Before nominating a Justice of the Supreme Court, the president of the United States must first way the qualifications of the candidates. Congress must then approve the nomination. ¶ a justice must be fare and unbiased with *(high)* principals. As you have probably red, the justice serves four life. Their are nine justices, won of whom is the cheif justice. When it meats, the Supreme Court may here many cases. The justices decides questions concerning the constitution, witch are of grate importance to the nation. ¶ Therefore, it is plane that the president's choice is of concern to everyone and requires much care.

CONTEXT CHECK

[What is the communication about?]

Directions: Following are 3 groups of sentences concerning the 2 letters and the report in this unit that you have keyed. Fill in the blanks; you may refer to the communications.

HELPFUL-HINT LETTER

1. The writer will be unable to help at the white elephant sale because he/she _____ .
2. For the sale the writer's mother has donated _____ .
3. The writer has asked Celia to stop by and _____ .

YOU'RE ON YOUR OWN—ASSIGNMENT NO. 1

1. The new computer room is being dedicated on _____ .
2. The topic of the guest speakers is _____ .
3. Before retiring Arthur Jason was the school's _____ .

YOU'RE ON YOUR OWN—ASSIGNMENT NO. 2

1. The Supreme Court is made up of _____ justices.
2. A justice of the Supreme Court serves for _____ .
3. After the president nominates a justice of the Supreme Court, he/she must be approved by _____ .

PROOFREADING ASSIGNMENT

Directions: Insert proofreader's marks to indicate corrections in the following paragraph. Here are the 6 marks that will have to be inserted.

≡	capitalize	i̠ saw ha̠nnah.	I saw Hannah.
◯	close up	in⁀terested	interested
⁄	delete (take out)	intereͤsted	interested
∧	insert	intͤrested	interested
#	insert space	I#am interested.	I am interested.
⸢⸤	move left	Tell me about it. ⎡ I am interested.	Tell me about it. I am interested.

Near my school there are two home less cats. I

feed them eachday and am trying to find homes fore

them. do you know of anyone who would lke a grey

cat and a white cat?

5 Commas

Performance Objective:

Upon completion of this unit, you will be able to identify parenthetical expressions, appositive words and phrases, and direct address; and you will be able to apply the comma rules for parenthetical expressions, appositive words and phrases, and direct address.

5-1 PARENTHETICAL EXPRESSIONS (INTERRUPTING WORDS)

Sometimes we interrupt the main thought of a sentence and put in a word or phrase that adds no meaning to the sentence. A parenthetical expression, or interrupting word or phrase, that is not necessary to the meaning of a sentence is set off by commas. If the interrupting word or phrase occurs at the beginning or end of a sentence, only one comma is necessary.

Here is a list of words or phrases that are often used as parenthetical expressions:

as you know	indeed	of course
besides	in my opinion	on the other hand
by the way	needless to say	therefore
fortunately	nevertheless	to say the least
however	no doubt	to tell the truth
in addition	obviously	unfortunately

> In my opinion, your answer is not correct.
> We have, therefore, an extra ticket.
> The store closes at 6:00 p.m., as you know.

When the interrupting word or phrase is necessary to the meaning of the sentence, it should not be set off by commas.

> On the other hand, there is a strong possibility that we will win.
> *BUT*
> He wore a diamond ring on one hand and a gold ring on the other hand.

> To tell the truth, I am glad that we did not go today.
> *BUT*
> One ought to tell the truth at all times.

HINT: To help you decide whether an interrupting word or phrase is necessary to the meaning of a sentence, read the sentence without these words. If the sentence makes sense without the word or phrase, set off the interrupting expression by commas.

Directions: Rekey the following sentences, inserting commas wherever necessary.

1. If you arrive early however you will get a better seat.
2. I have no doubt in my mind that he is guilty.
3. Fortunately the snow stopped before we left.
4. The bouquet of roses is indeed beautiful.
5. His speech was too long in my opinion.

5-2 APPOSITIVES (DESCRIPTIVE WORDS)

An appositive is a word or phrase that immediately follows a noun and describes or explains the noun. Such a descriptive word or phrase is set off by commas. If the descriptive word or phrase occurs at the end of a sentence, only one comma is necessary.

Edna Best, our tour guide, took us everywhere. (The descriptive words, *our tour guide*, explain who Edna Best is.)

Our history teacher, Mrs. Muldoon, returned the test papers. (The descriptive words, *Mrs. Muldoon*, identify the teacher.)

My favorite magazine, TEEN REVIEW, is not in the library. (The descriptive words, *TEEN REVIEW*, identify the magazine.)

Exception: Appositives of only one word are not set off by commas.

My friend Corrie sent me a birthday card.
Our brother Bobbie was best man at the wedding.

TRY-OUT EXERCISE

Directions: Rekey the following sentences, inserting commas wherever necessary.

1. Dr. Mapes my dentist found two cavities in my teeth.
2. Can you see my brother Herman in that crowd?
3. Our assigned book CONSTITUTIONAL CRISES is difficult to read.
4. The television announcer Robert Rose has a pleasant voice.
5. Arlene's sister Selma enlisted in the Army.

5-3 ADDITIONAL DESCRIPTIVE OR EXPLANATORY EXPRESSIONS

The *month and date* are set off by commas when they follow the day of the week.

Wednesday, August 15, is my birthday.

The *year* is set off by commas when it follows the month and date.

Kelly was born on November 1, 1981, and is the youngest in the family.

The name of a *state* is set off by commas when it follows the name of a city.

We drove to Orlando, Florida, to visit Disney World.

Directions: Rekey the following sentences, inserting commas wherever necessary.

1. My dental appointments are on Monday May 6 and on May 12.
2. Our uncle has lived in Tacoma Washington for three years.
3. Jerry and Alice were married on June 1 1975 and have four children.
4. We are leaving for Paris France on Monday July 7.
5. After his graduation on June 23 1986 Sal moved to Canton Ohio.

5-4
DIRECT ADDRESS

When you speak or write to someone and call that person by name or title, that is direct address. Names and titles in direct address are set off by commas. If direct address occurs at the beginning or end of a sentence, only one comma is necessary.

I think, Jasper, that it is time to leave.
Ladies and gentlemen, please be seated.
Is this your umbrella, sir?
Dr. Callahan, what is your diagnosis?

**TRY-OUT
EXERCISE**

Directions: Rekey the following sentences, inserting commas wherever necessary.

1. Do you work after school Freddie?
2. I believe sir that you are in my seat.
3. Miss Diaz please autograph my book.
4. On our way to the theater girls let's stop for lunch.
5. Would you Mr. Amato reconsider your decision?

SENTENCE EXERCISE

Directions: Rekey the following sentences in the spaces provided, inserting commas wherever necessary.

EXAMPLE:

Obviously the sign was placed there by the dean Mrs. Rogers.

Obviously, the sign was placed there by the dean, Mrs. Rogers.

1. We have no doubt that the Giants our favorite team will win.

_____

2. Ladies and gentlemen this is your pilot speaking; we will arrive in Memphis Tennessee at 8:00 p.m.

_____

_____

3. My family and I visited Newport Rhode Island on December 29 1986 and needless to say enjoyed visiting the old mansions.

_____

_____

4. Fortunately our math teacher Mr. Jenkins has agreed to become the club's adviser.

_____

_____

5. Larry I don't feel like going; besides it is raining.

_____

6. You will of course receive your award at the assembly on Friday June 25.

_____

7. My sister Tillie was married on May 17 1987 and has lived in San Francisco California ever since.

_____

_____

8. Tell me Alma weren't you ever taught to tell the truth?

_____

9. I asked Ms. Nadler the librarian if I could reserve my favorite book A TALE OF TWO CITIES.

_____

_____

10. As you know my brother Saul is starting a new job today.

_____

DICTIONARY USAGE

Directions: Here are the more difficult words and their meanings that appear in the assignments in this unit. Study them carefully; complete the sentences that follow.

besides	in addition; moreover
extravagance	an excessive or wasteful spending of money
figurehead	the head of a country with no real authority or responsibility
intrigued (to be _____ by)	to be curious or interested
newsworthy	interesting enough to report
nuptials	a wedding of great importance; for example, a royal wedding
nutrition	food, nourishment
pique (verb)	arouse
reference (noun)	material that is read or consulted for information
subscribe	to place an order for a number of issues of a magazine

Directions for completing the following sentences: Select the appropriate word from the above list, and key it in each blank.

1. Good _____ is essential to good health.
2. Would you care to _____ to a fashion magazine for one year?
3. Helene went to the library for a book to use as a _____ for the report she is writing.
4. The ghostly sounds coming from the empty house certainly _____ _____ my curiosity.
5. The royal _____ took place in Monaco at the castle of the bridegroom.
6. I was too lazy to go out on Saturday; _____, I had a cold.
7. Years ago the British king or queen had absolute power; today he or she is a _____.
8. That newspaper prints any story that is _____.
9. I am _____ by a strange story that I read in the newspaper this morning, and I would like to find out more about it.
10. Fran would not spend money on a fancy dress to be worn only one time; she considers that a great _____.

Directions Key this personal-business letter in block style with open punctuation. You are to insert the following comma usages: 3 interrupting words or phrases (4 commas), 2 appositives (3 commas), 2 explanatory expressions (3 commas), and 1 direct address (1 comma).

Use a full sheet of paper
Margins: 50-space line (elite 26-81, pica 17-72)

All parts of the letter are to be keyed at the left margin. Key your return address on the 13th line from the top edge of the paper; the date is on line 15 under your two-line return address. Quadruple-space after the date, and key the inside address (name and address of person to whom the letter is going). Double-space; key the salutation. Double-space after the salutation, and single-space the body. Double-space after the body; key the complimentary close. Quadruple-space, and key your name.

Your street address
Your city, state ZIP
April 30, 19--

Mr. John Espino, Editor
GOOD NUTRITION
1400 Melrose Avenue
Cincinnati, OH 45227-2802

Dear Mr. Espino

My health teacher Ms. Cerra has given the class an assignment: to write a report on nutrition.

Of course there are many approaches to that topic. I have decided to make up menus for one week that consist of well-balanced meals.

Mr. Espino my parents subscribe to your magazine GOOD NUTRITION. The April 6 19-- issue contained several menus for good health. I would like to use them as reference for my report, which is due on Tuesday May 14. Unfortunately I cannot find our copy of the magazine at home and therefore would appreciate your sending me another copy.

Please let me know if there is a charge.

Sincerely yours

Your name

Directions Key this personal note in modified block style with open punctuation. Insert commas wherever necessary.

Use a full sheet of paper.
Margins: 50-space line (elite 26-81; pica 17-72)
Tabs and center points: Elite 51; pica 42

Key the date at the center of the 15th line from the top edge of the paper. Quadruple-space, and key the salutation. Double-space after the salutation, and single-space the body. Double-space after the body; key the complimentary close at the center point of the paper.

November 7, 19--

Dear Sammy

¶ Open-school activities will take place at our school on Tuesday November 16. Therefore letters have been sent to our parents inviting them to visit.

¶ Sammy I am a little worried. I know that my math teacher Ms. Jacobs will tell my parents that I did not hand in several homework assignments. Unfortunately I just forgot about my homework on those days. Besides I had left my books in school.

¶ My parents of course will be angry. In addition my favorite uncle David Stern promised me a new bicycle if I earned a straight "A" average. I have no doubt that I will not receive an "A" in math.

¶ I wish that I could be like my sister Janie; she has never missed a homework assignment.

Sincerely

Directions Key the following short report, inserting commas wherever necessary.

Use a full sheet of paper.
Margins: 60-space line (elite 21-86; pica 12-77)
Tabs: Elite 26; pica 17
Center points: Elite 51; pica 42

Center the title (KEY IN ALL CAPITAL LETTERS) on line 12 from the top edge of the paper for elite and line 10 for pica. Quadruple-space to the first paragraph. Double-space the report. Indent paragraphs 5 spaces.

THE SPORT OF ROYALTY WATCHING

We are always intrigued by royalty. There are of course few monarchs left; and those who remain pique the interest of the world.

A royal marriage is to say the least newsworthy. However there is no doubt that the marriage of a commoner to a prince or princess captures world headlines. For example the nuptials of Britain's Charles and Di on July 29 1981 were front-page news. Diana a real-life fairy princess became the toast of England. Headlines were made again when Diana had her first child William.

People still remember when the movie star Grace Kelly married Monaco's ruler Prince Rainier. Unfortunately Princess Grace died several years ago in a tragic automobile accident.

Today's monarchs are figureheads; they have little power. Nevertheless we still like to read about them and their extravagances. Perhaps we dream of ourselves in their places.

CONTEXT CHECK

[What is the
communication about?]

Directions: Following are 3 groups of sentences concerning the 2 letters and the report in this unit that you have keyed. Fill in the blanks; you may refer to the communications.

HELPFUL-HINT LETTER

1. The class assignment is to write a report on _____
   _____ .

2. The report is due on _____ .
3. The writer's parents subscribe to _____ .

YOU'RE ON YOUR OWN—ASSIGNMENT NO. 1

1. Open-school activities will take place on _____ .
2. The writer is worried because he/she did not _____
   _____ .

3. Does the writer think that he/she will now receive the bicycle promised by Uncle David for a straight "A" average? Yes_____
   No_____

YOU'RE ON YOUR OWN—ASSIGNMENT NO. 2

1. The British wedding that captured world headlines was that of _____ and _____ .
2. The royal couple's first-born son was named _____
   _____ .

3. The movie star, _____ , was married to _____ of Monaco.

PROOFREADING ASSIGNMENT

Directions: Insert proofreader's marks to indicate corrections in the following paragraph. Here are the 6 marks that will have to be inserted.

≡	capitalize	i̲ broke it.	I broke it.
⊂	close up	op portunity	opportunity
#	insert space	We sawhim	We saw him.
∿	transpose	cheif	chief
⊙	insert period	Watch him ⊙	Watch him.
/	lowercase letter	Look at This.	Look at this.

The day after thanks giving is the biggest shopping dayof the yaer. There is a joyful feeling in the air Santa is busy making final Preparations for his ride on the night before Christmas.

6 Commas (Concluded)

Performance Objective:

Upon completion of this unit, you will be able to identify a series of items, an introductory phrase or clause, and two independent clauses separated by a conjunction; and you will be able to apply their comma rules.

6-1
SERIES

Use commas to separate three or more items in a series. The word *and* usually appears before the last item in a series; place a comma before it.

Today I took tests in English, history, and math.
Keeley, Millie, Juan, and Jose were standing on the line.
Don't forget to wash the dishes, shovel the snow, and walk the dog.

TRY-OUT EXERCISE

Directions: Rekey the following sentences, inserting commas wherever necessary.

1. We bought a dozen rolls six cupcakes a loaf of bread and a pie for Mrs. Mansfield.
2. Let's invite Ray Carlos and Herman to join us for lunch.
3. My friend Annie has two dogs three cats a turtle and a rabbit.
4. I like to play baseball football and basketball.
5. Jay has to clean the car change his clothes pick up the tickets and meet us by five o'clock.

6-2
INTRODUCTORY EXPRESSIONS

An introductory phrase or clause appears at the beginning of a sentence; it is separated from the rest of the sentence by a comma. Here are some of the words that are used to introduce such a phrase or clause.

after	during	unless
although	if	when
as	in	while
because	on	

While attending college at night, I worked during the day.
In a matter of minutes, the firemen arrived.
Because today is a holiday, the stores are closed.

When the phrase or clause appears within the sentence and not at the beginning, it is not set off by commas.

I worked during the day while attending college at night.
The firemen arrived in a matter of minutes.
The stores are closed because today is a holiday.

A short introductory phrase does not usually require a comma.

On Tuesday we are moving to Chicago.
On June 15 I hope to graduate.

TRY-OUT EXERCISE

Directions: Rekey the following sentences, inserting commas wherever necessary.

1. When you are feeling better please visit us.
2. Because of the many absentees no vote could be taken.
3. Don't tell me you're sorry if you don't mean it.
4. In July we are leaving for a short vacation.
5. Unless you are truthful now I won't trust you again.

BRIEF GRAMMAR REVIEW

Let's review two important parts of speech: the subject and the verb. A sentence must contain at least one subject and at least one verb. The subject is the person, place, or thing that the sentence is about. The verb expresses the action of the subject. In the following examples, the subject(s) is underscored one time; the verb(s) is underscored twice.

Sal hurt his arm.
My sister and I love the seashore.
Park Avenue is a wide street.
The girl laughed and cried at the same time.

6-3 CONJUNCTIONS

An independent clause contains a subject and a verb; it can stand alone as a sentence. A comma separates two independent clauses that are joined by *and, or, but* or *nor.*

Gene arrived late, and he missed the beginning of the movie.
The girl stumbled, but she kept her balance.
Eat your dinner, and go to bed early.

The third example above is an imperative sentence or command; the subject of each independent clause is the implied *you.*

If *and, or, but,* or *nor* does not join two independent clauses, no comma is placed before *and, or, but,* or *nor.*

Gene arrived late and missed the beginning of the movie.
The girl stumbled but kept her balance.

Each of the two foregoing sentences contains only one independent clause (an independent clause contains both a subject and a verb). Therefore, no comma is placed before *and* or *but.*

TRY-OUT EXERCISE

Directions: Rekey the following sentences, inserting commas wherever necessary.

1. We visited the artist in his studio and we watched him work.
2. I can understand your reasoning but do not agree with you.
3. Dry your tears and tell me your problems.
4. Jack and Jill went up the hill and fetched the water.
5. Ronnie is an expert mechanic but he doesn't like his job.

SENTENCE EXERCISE

Directions: Rekey the following sentences in the spaces provided, inserting commas wherever necessary. If a sentence requires no comma(s), key *correct* in the space below it.

EXAMPLE:

When I visited the zoo I saw the reptiles elephants seals and pandas.

When I visited the zoo, I saw the reptiles, elephants, seals, and pandas.

1. Our class went on a picnic today but Pete was too sick to go.

_____

2. Rolinda ran for the bus and missed it by one minute.

_____

3. As I walked into the room I was surprised to see Laura Doris Mavis and Sue.

_____

4. You must make up your mind or you will lose the opportunity to vote.

_____

5. Until my father was hired by his current employer he worked 20 miles away.

_____

6. Try to get there early and save a seat for me.

_____

7. On Monday we are having a special assembly of freshmen juniors and sophomores.

_____

_____

8. Terry is staying at the hotel until tomorrow because there are no flights available today.

_____

_____

9. We won't wait any longer to see Mr. Epps nor will we return.

_____

10. During Beth's visit to a farm this summer she fed the chickens rode a horse and milked the cows.

_____

_____

DICTIONARY USAGE

Directions: Here are the more difficult words and their meanings that appear in the assignments in this unit. Study them carefully; complete the sentences that follow.

circulation (of a magazine)	the number of copies of each issue distributed to readers
collision	coming violently into contact; a crash
defray	to pay
excess (adjective)	more than what is necessary
issue (noun) (_____ of a magazine)	the total quantity printed at one time; example: December issue
local (adjective)	referring to some small area rather than a widespread one; serving a limited area
maiden voyage	a ship's first sailing
perish	to die
route (noun)	a line of travel
subscription	an order for a number of issues of a magazine; example: a one-year subscription

Directions for completing the following sentences: Select the appropriate word from the above list, and key it in each blank.

1. I will give you directions for coming to my house by an easy _____ _____ .

2. From the quart of milk, fill these two glasses; pour the _____ _____ milk into a pitcher.

3. During the violent earthquake in the town, 100 people _____ _____ .

4. For my birthday Jamie gave me a one-year _____ to a sports magazine.

5. The two cars were traveling at a very fast speed; unfortunately, there was a _____ in which three people were hurt.

6. My father gave me $10 to help _____ the cost of my class jacket.

7. The _____ merchants decided to run a one-day sidewalk sale.

8. My brother is the editor of a new magazine; since last year its ___ _____ doubled to one million readers.

9. I think that the April _____ of TIME is now on the newsstands.

10. One thousand passengers were aboard the brand new ship as she set sail on her _____ .

Directions: Key this personal-business letter in block style with open punctuation. You are to insert the following comma usages: 1 series, 3 introductory, and 2 conjunctions.

Use a full sheet of paper.
Margins: 50-space line (elite 26-81; pica 17-72)

All parts of the letter are to be keyed at the left margin. Key your return address on the 13th line from the top edge of the paper; the date is on line 15 under your two-line return address. Quadruple-space after the date, and key the inside address (name and address of person to whom the letter is going). Double-space; key the salutation. Double-space after the salutation, and single-space the body. Double-space after the body; key the complimentary close. Quadruple-space, and key your name.

Your street address
Your city, state   ZIP
October 1, 19--

Ms. Helene Vega, Manager
The Hidden Boutique
130 North Jackson Street
Topeka, KS   66603-9654

Dear Ms. Vega

Would you care to place an ad in our school newspaper? As you may be aware local merchants like to
advertise in THE MONITOR. We publish two issues a
year and advertising rates are low. If you place an
ad before October 30 you will receive a special rate.

Income from advertising helps defray the cost of
printing and any excess funds are used to buy food
for needy families in town.

We are proud of our efforts and boast a large cir-
culation. THE MONITOR is read by our friends neighbors parents and relatives. With the Christmas
season approaching an ad should bring additional
business.

I would be happy to stop by to help you place your ad.

Cordially yours

Your name

Directions: Key this personal note in modified block style with mixed punctuation. Insert commas wherever necessary.

Use a full sheet of paper.
Margins: 50-space line (elite 26-81; pica 17-72)
Tabs and center points: Elite 51; pica 42

Key the date at the center of the 15th line from the top edge of the paper. Quadruple-space, and key the salutation. Double-space after the salutation, and single-space the body. Double-space after the body; key the complimentary close at the center point of the paper.

June 22, 19--

Dear Hector:

I just won a radio for selling the most magazine
subscriptions on my route and had to tell you.

I sell subscriptions to HOW TO DO IT YOURSELF and
I enjoy doing it. The magazine practically sells
itself. Although it appears only four times a year
each issue is filled with valuable information.
The price is rather high but people save a lot of
money by following the do-it-yourself instructions.

Magazine subscriptions are ideal for gift giving
because you don't have to worry about fit size or
color.

Have a great summer and try to write soon. If you
would like a magazine subscription let me know.

Sincerely,

Directions: Key the following short report, inserting commas wherever necessary. Refer to page 5 for a review of proofreader's marks.

Use a full sheet of paper.
Margins: 60-space line (elite 21-86; pica 12-77)
Tabs: Elite 26; pica 17
Center points: Elite 51; pica 42

Center the title on line 12 from the top edge of the paper for elite and line 10 for pica. Quadruple-space to the first paragraph. Double-space the report. Indent paragraphs 5 spaces.

NOTE: You will not be able to copy this report line for line. Use your judgment as to where each line should end within the margins given.

Center   *Quadruple space*

The Titanic

After a collision with an iceberg in 1912 the luxury steamships Titanic

sank. She was considered unsinkable but she sank on her maiden voyage.

Her passengers included millionaires titled aristocrats and

im migrants.   ¶   The Titanic was a floating palace but did not have enough

lifeboats. when she finally went down 1,500 men women and children

perished with her.   ¶   Another ship was not too far away but it did

not hear the Titanic's distress calls and its radio was not turned on.

   ¶   This was a terrible tragedy and it taught the world an important

lesson. There is no unsinkable ship.

CONTEXT CHECK
[What is the
communication about?]

Directions: Following are 3 groups of sentences concerning the 2 letters and the report in this unit that you have keyed. Fill in the blanks; you may refer to the communications.

HELPFUL-HINT LETTER

1. The name of the school newspaper is _____.
2. How many issues are published each year? _____
3. Excess income from advertising is used to _____.

YOU'RE ON YOUR OWN—ASSIGNMENT NO. 1

1. The writer is selling subscriptions to the magazine entitled _____
   _____.

2. People who subscribe to the publication can save money by _____
   _____.

3. Magazine subscriptions are ideal for gift giving because you don't have to worry about _____.

YOU'RE ON YOUR OWN—ASSIGNMENT NO. 2

1. The *Titanic* sank in 1912 after _____.
2. The *Titanic* was mistakenly considered to be _____
   _____.

3. A neighboring ship did not hear the *Titanic's* distress calls because
   _____.

PROOFREADING ASSIGNMENT

Directions: Insert proofreader's marks to indicate corrections in the following paragraph. Here are the 6 marks that will have to be inserted.

mark		
close up	book let	booklet
delete	noteed	noted
insert space	Hewon the prize.	He won the prize.
lowercase letter	Grade	grade
move left	Jane is coming. June is not.	Jane is coming. June is not.
transpose	recieve	receive

My family has a subscriptions to the daily newspaper.

Every Evening my father readsthe sports page, my

mother reads the thaeter and fashion pages, and

I like to solve the cross word puzzle.

Review Lesson Units 4-6

NAME_____

SENTENCE REVIEW

Directions: Rekey the following sentences in the spaces provided, inserting commas and correcting the homonyms wherever necessary.

EXAMPLE:

Needless to say I will weight four you.

Needless to say, I will wait for you.

1. The principle Ms. Fuller asked me to male her letters.

_____

2. Don't take that rode therefore because of the ice.

_____

3. March 11 1988 was the date on witch my brother Johnny was born.

_____

4. I have no doubt Tom that you will call when your plain lands.

_____

5. The first noise I herd of course was the peel of the bell.

_____

6. The circus came to town this passed weak and our hole family went to see it.

_____

7. Ginny McGuire my sister's friend has blue eyes read hair and a dimple in her chin.

_____

_____

8. On Friday June 6 my father flu to Boise Idaho on business.

_____

9. I guest the exact amount of marbles in the jar and won $10.

_____

10. During our visit to the zoo I fed the bares the seals and the monkeys.

_____

11. Karen felt week after having the flew but she went to school.

_____

12. On the other hand Betsy you are not being fare.

_____

13. Although you told me to great the onion into the meat I forgot too do it.

_____

14. Frank we must have lost our way because we have past threw here before.

_____

15. Cut the cake now and save me a peace.

_____

Directions Rekey this personal note in modified block style with open punctuation. Use a full sheet of paper with a 50-space line. Insert commas, and correct homonyms wherever necessary.

November 10, 19--

Dear Lenny

At the beginning of this month the home of our neighbors the Blakes was badly burned in a fire.. Unfortunately they lost most of there possessions.

Our school's principle started a fire fund and asked for donations of money clothing and services. Lenny everyone came threw with all kinds of help.

The for Blake children soon had new clothing and the hole town helped rebuild their house. Repairmen worked on the house 24 ours a day; in to weeks it was ready to be lived in.

This is a grate town in witch to live; people take care of one another.

Sincerely

Directions   Key this personal note in block style with open punctuation. Use a full sheet of paper with a 60-space line. Insert commas, and correct homonyms wherever necessary.

February 9, 19--

Dear Bobbie

When my for brothers and I used to speak of our baby sister Wendy it was definitely not in endearing terms. Therefore at first we did not worry when she became ill won weak ago.

Soon we grew fearful that she might not recover and we would grown whenever we herd her cry. Our ant flu in from Chicago Illinois witch is most unusual.

Yesterday the doctor told us that Wendy wood get better and she is now on the rode to recovery. Today she ate a peace of cake pulled the dog's tale and through her toys on the floor. She is her old self.

Bobbie my brothers and I have promised ourselves that we will never complain about Wendy again--until next month.

Sincerely

PROOFREADING REVIEW

Directions Insert proofreader's marks to indicate corrections in the following paragraph. Here are the 6 marks that will have to be inserted.

☰	capitalize	Hello, cindy.	Hello, Cindy.
◡	close up	walk ing	walking
⋀	insert	br͜very	bravery
⊙	insert period	I'm ready⊙	I'm ready.
⊏	move left	Let's not go. I'm ill.	Let's not go. I'm ill.
∿	transpose	reciept	receipt

Last summer I was a lifegaurd at a local pool. Most day were quite routine one day, however, my job became very important. Some one would have drowned if I had not rescued him. I felt good after having saved a life.

7 Colon and Semicolon

Performance Objective:

Upon completion of this unit, you will be able to apply the rules for usage of the colon and semicolon in written communications.

7-1
COLON

As you have already learned in your keyboarding class, a colon may be placed after the salutation in a business letter.

Dear Mr. Ryan: Dear Mrs. Loring:
Ladies and Gentlemen: Dear Ms. Martin:

Use a colon after the words *as follows* or *the following* when several items are listed. Space two times after the colon.

You will need the following supplies for your art class: a ruler, three paint brushes, and a drawing pen.

For breakfast I had the following: orange juice, two slices of toast, two eggs, and a glass of milk.

Use a colon between the hours and minutes when expressing time. Leave *no* space before or after the colon.

The dance will begin at 8:30 this evening.
I missed the 10:00 bus.

TRY-OUT EXERCISE

Directions Rekey the following sentences, inserting colons wherever necessary.

1. The Sunday movie schedule is as follows 12 00, 1 15, 2 30, and 3 45.
2. The train arrived at 10 30 instead of 10 00.
3. The following people will be on the committee Annette, Shandai, Bernadette, and Rachelle.
4. You must be here by 6 45 p.m. sharp.
5. Please shop for the following items for dinner potatoes, rice, and grapefruit.

7-2
SEMICOLON BETWEEN INDEPENDENT CLAUSES

In Unit 6 we learned that an independent clause contains at least one subject and one verb; it can stand alone as a sentence. A comma separates two independent clauses that are connected by *and*, *or*, *but*, or *nor*.

Team members must pass this test, or they will not play on Saturday.
Chuck mailed the letter, and he received a reply in two days.
Cora and Laura arrived early, but they left late.

When one or both of the independent clauses contain a comma or commas, place a semicolon before the connecting word.

As you know, team members must pass this test; or they will not play on Saturday.

Chuck mailed the letter; and he received a reply on Monday, June 2.

Cora, Dora, and Laura arrived early; but they left late.

TRY-OUT EXERCISE

Directions: Rekey the following sentences, inserting semicolons wherever necessary.

1. On my way here, I ate ice cream and I'm not hungry now.
2. Penny invited her entire family to her wedding but not all of her aunts, uncles, and cousins are able to attend.
3. Marvinia, call us when your plane lands or we will worry.
4. Our landlady, Mrs. Morris, is raising our rent and we will move.
5. I would like to borrow your umbrella but I will return it, of course.

7-3
SEMICOLON TO REPLACE A CONNECTING WORD

When the connecting word (*and*, *or*, *but*, or *nor*) is omitted, use a semicolon to separate two closely related independent clauses.

Two team members did not pass the test; they will not play on Saturday.

Chuck mailed the letter; he received a reply in two days.

The girls arrived early; they left late.

TRY-OUT EXERCISE

Directions: Rekey the following sentences, inserting semicolons wherever necessary.

1. I like to ice skate I want to take lessons.
2. The ice is not frozen we cannot skate today.
3. Sandy fell on the ice she broke her arm.
4. My mother is knitting me a heavy sweater it will be finished soon.
5. The room was cold we lit a fire.

7-4
SEMICOLON BEFORE A TRANSITIONAL WORD OR PHRASE

In Unit 5 we learned that parenthetical expressions (interrupting words or phrases) are not necessary to the meaning of a sentence and are set off by commas. Examples of these parenthetical expressions follow:

besides	however	of course
for example	meanwhile	otherwise
(un)fortunately	nevertheless	therefore

My sister pays her dues regularly, of course.

Gaby, therefore, will return to school this week.

Besides, I didn't like the color.

These parenthetical expressions are called transitional words or phrases when they connect two independent clauses; place a semicolon before the transitional word or phrase and a comma after it.

My sister is a member of the club; <u>of course</u>, she pays her dues on time.

Gaby is feeling better; <u>therefore</u>, she will return to school this week.

I returned the boots that were tight; <u>besides</u>, I didn't like the color.

TRY-OUT EXERCISE

Directions: Rekey the following sentences, inserting semicolons and commas wherever necessary.

1. I received a computer for my birthday however I don't know how to use it yet.
2. My brother enlisted in the Navy of course we are going to miss him.
3. Her dentist told Sheila to stop eating sweets nevertheless she eats candy every day.
4. The parade will be canceled in case of rain otherwise it will take place this Sunday.
5. Aunt Ida is always traveling for example she just returned from Japan.

SENTENCE EXERCISE

Directions: Rekey the following sentences in the spaces provided, inserting colons, semicolons, and commas wherever necessary.

EXAMPLE:

The meeting began at 10 00 however it was over by 10 30.

The meeting began at 10:00; however, it was over by 10:30.

1. Santa packed his sleigh on Monday evening, December 24 and he was off to make his deliveries around the world.

_____

_____

2. The dog barked loudly the burglar fled.

_____

3. The following people volunteered for the job of class secretary Loriann, Flavia, Maggie, and Derek.

_____

_____

4. I would like to get a part-time job after 3 00 each afternoon of course I can work full time during the summer.

_____

_____

5. Lorraine, let's catch the 12 00 show or we will have to pay more for the 1 30 show.

_____

_____

6. I just replaced my typewriter ribbon fortunately I had an extra one on hand.

_____

7. As you know, the fire was put out by 9 45 but we had smoke damage.

_____

8. Please give me a 2 00 appointment I can't be there before that time.

_____

9. Soldiers are stationed all over the world for example my brother is stationed in Greece.

_____

_____

10. The butcher received a shipment of the following items veal, lamb, beef, and pork.

_____

_____

DICTIONARY USAGE

Directions Here are the more difficult words and their meanings that appear in the assignments in this unit. Study them carefully; complete the sentences that follow:

besides	in addition; moreover
fiendish	wicked; cruel
miniature (adjective)	very small
nevertheless	in spite of that
peal (verb)	to ring loudly
plight (noun)	a distressing situation
realm	kingdom
souvenir	something kept as a reminder; a memento
unique	the only one; very unusual
vow (verb)	to make a solemn promise

Directions for completing the following sentences: Select the appropriate word from the above list, and key it in each blank.

1. Your watch is _____ ; I have never seen another one like it.
2. Amid much rejoicing, the bells _____ to announce that the _____ witch was dead.
3. The artist makes _____ copies of masterpieces; he puts in all the details of the larger pictures.
4. It is snowing heavily; _____ , my brother drove to school to pick me up.
5. I pity the _____ of the man who just missed his bus and has to wait an hour in a pouring rain for another one.
6. On the occasion of the royal marriage, the bells will _____ all over the _____ .
7. I bought a picture of the Empire State Building as a _____ of our visit to New York City.
8. The bride and groom _____ to love and honor each other.
9. Your uncle's car is _____ ; there are not many black cars with green fenders.
10. We refused to pay the plumber for the poor work he did; _____ _____ , the job was never completed.

HELPFUL-HINT LETTER

Directions: Key this personal note in block style with open punctuation. You are to insert the following punctuation usages: 2 colons, 6 semicolons, and 2 commas after transitional words.

Use a full sheet of paper.
Margins: 50-space line (elite 26-81; pica 17-72)

All parts of the note are to be keyed at the left margin. Key the date on the 15th line from the top edge of the paper. Quadruple-space, and key the salutation. Double-space after the salutation, and single-space the body. Double-space after the body; key the complimentary close.

December 10, 19--

Dear Danielle

On Saturday, December 3, I saw The Nutcracker and I loved it. Children enjoy this ballet however there were also a lot of adults in the audience enjoying themselves.

I went with my mother, sister, and godmother and we met my father at the theater. We had lunch at 12 00 the ballet began at 2 00.

The entire afternoon was like a dream besides my father bought me a pair of miniature ballet slippers as a souvenir.

Danielle, you should see this ballet. Unfortunately, you have only until January 3 or you will miss it.

I hope to see you during the Christmas vacation.

Sincerely

Directions: Key the following short report. Insert colons, semicolons, and commas wherever necessary.

Use a full sheet of paper.
Margins: 60-space line (elite 21-86; pica 12-77)
Tabs: Elite 26; pica 17
Center points: Elite 51; pica 42

Center the title (KEY IN ALL CAPITAL LETTERS) on the 12th line from the top edge of the paper for elite and the 10th line for pica. Quadruple-space to the first paragraph. Double-space the report. Indent paragraphs 5 spaces.

THE KING AND THE DRAGON

Once upon a time, there was a handsome king and he ruled The Land of Good Deeds. He was very unhappy indeed he was miserable because he had no queen. The young ladies of his realm did not interest him besides he was looking for someone so perfect that she did not appear to exist.

One day a beggar traveled through the realm and he told about the most beautiful princess in the world, Cindy Ella. She lived in the next realm, The Land of the Fiendish Dragon but she was a prisoner of the dragon.

The king heard of her plight and vowed to do the following slay the dragon, free Cindy Ella, ask for her hand in marriage, and make her his queen. He bravely left on his mission.

This is a fairy tale therefore the ending is a happy one. The king slew the dragon he married Cindy Ella. On a very beautiful Sunday morning at 11 00 in The Land of Good Deeds, the bells pealed loudly as Cindy Ella became his queen.

YOU'RE ON YOUR OWN— ASSIGNMENT NO. 2

Directions: Key the personal-business letter on page 80 in modified block style with indented paragraphs and mixed punctuation. Insert colons, semicolons, and commas wherever necessary.

Use a full sheet of paper.
Margins: 60-space line (elite 21-86; pica 12-77)
Tabs: Elite 26, 51; pica 17, 42
Center points: Elite 51; pica 42

Key your return address at the center of the 13th line from the top edge of the paper; the date is on line 15 under your two-line return address. Quadruple-space after the date, and key the inside address (name and address of person to whom the letter is going). Double-space; key the salutation. Double-space after the salutation, and single-space the body. Double-space after the body; key the complimentary close at the center point. Quadruple-space, and key your name at the center point.

NOTE: You will not be able to copy this letter line for line. Use your judgment as to where each line should end within the margins given.

Your street address
Your city, state Zip
April 1, 19--

Ms. Fanny Cortes
Shopping Service
Moraine's Department Store
360 Brisbane Street
Memphis, TN 38104-8512

Dear Ms. Cortes:
⁋ My sister Sylvia is having an engagement party on Saturday, May 10 and I would like to order a gift for her.
⁋ I can spend only $20 nevertheless I hope that you can help me choose something for her. I was thinking of any one of the following items a toaster, a can opener, a cake dish, or an iron. I know, Ms. Cortes, that these are not unique gifts but perhaps you can select something else that is. If necessary I could borrow additional money from my parents however I would rather not have to do this.
⁋ Please let me know the cost of the gift you select I will mail you the payment.

Sincerely yours,

Your name

CONTEXT CHECK

[What is the communication about?]

Directions: Following are three groups of sentences concerning the two letters and the report in this unit that you have keyed. Fill in the blanks; you may refer to the communications.

HELPFUL-HINT LETTER

1. The writer saw the ballet entitled _____.
2. The writer received as a souvenir a pair of _____.
3. The ballet will be performed only until _____.

YOU'RE ON YOUR OWN—ASSIGNMENT NO. 1

1. The king was miserable because he had _____.
2. Princess Cindy Ella was a prisoner of the _____.
3. The king slew the dragon, and he _____ Cindy Ella.

YOU'RE ON YOUR OWN—ASSIGNMENT NO. 2

1. Sylvia's engagement party will take place on _____ _____ .
2. For Sylvia's gift the writer can spend only _____.
3. One of the items that the writer is considering as a gift for Sylvia is _____ .

Directions: Insert proofreader's marks to indicate corrections in the following paragraph. Here are the 6 marks that will have to be inserted.

≡	capitalize	i lost it.	I lost it.
◠	close up	puz zle	puzzle
✗	delete	autoomobile	automobile
⋀	insert	autmobile	automobile
⊙	insert period	Come today I need you.	Come today. I need you.
/	lowercase letter	Please Try.	Please try.

I love mystery sto ries. I especially like those by
Agatha Christie. Her detective is Named Hercule Poirot he
is alwys able to solves any kind of murder. I think that I
would like to write a mystery story.

8 The Apostrophe

Performance Objective:

Upon completion of this unit, you will be able to apply the rules for making singular and plural nouns possessive and for forming contractions in written communications.

8-1
POSSESSION: SINGULAR NOUNS

(*Reminder:* A noun is a person, place, or thing. A singular noun is *one* person, place, or thing.) To make a singular noun possessive, add an apostrophe and an s ('s).

the girl's coat	the boss's secretary
the traveler's passport	Tess's desk
Rita's radio	Mr. Cox's mistake
the lady's wristwatch	the governess's uniform

TRY-OUT EXERCISE

Directions: Rekey the following sentences, making possessive the words in parentheses.

1. The (plumber) helper arrived ten minutes late.
2. Meet us later at (Martin) house.
3. (Bess) baby is so cute.
4. The (countess) tiara was stolen.
5. Are you sure that the (passenger) ticket is lost?

8-2
POSSESSION: PLURAL NOUNS ENDING IN *S*

(*Reminder:* A plural noun is two or more persons, places, or things.) To make a plural noun ending in s possessive, place an apostrophe after the s (s').

the girls' coats	the governesses' uniforms
the Coxes' children	the Wiltons' new home
the ladies' wristwatches	the travelers' passports

TRY-OUT EXERCISE

Directions: Rekey the following sentences, making plural and possessive the words in parentheses.

1. Three (occupant) names are on the office door.
2. The (Fox) house will be put up for sale.
3. My (teacher) complaints about me included lateness.
4. Our (hostess) husbands danced with their wives.
5. All the (baby) mothers met in the park.

8-3
POSSESSION: PLURAL NOUNS NOT ENDING IN S

To make possessive a plural noun not ending in *s*, add an apostrophe and an *s* (*'s*).

the children's clothing
the men's exercise class
the women's dresses

Directions: Rekey the following sentences, making possessive the words in parentheses.

1. The (children) mother bought them each a new toy.
2. The actor received the (audience) applause.
3. The police calmed the (crowd) anger.
4. The (women) group meets every third Monday.
5. (People) wishes are expressed at the ballot box.

8-4
CONTRACTIONS

Sometimes we shorten certain words or phrases and, in so doing, drop one or more letters from their spelling. When we do this, the omission of the letter or letters is indicated by an apostrophe. Such a shortening of words is called a *contraction*. Examples are shown below.

cannot	= can't	it is	= it's*
did not	= didn't	let us	= let's
do not	= don't	there is	= there's
have not	= haven't	they have	= they've
I am	= I'm	was not	= wasn't
I will	= I'll	we are	= we're
is not	= isn't	would not	=wouldn't

*The possessive word *its* does not take the apostrophe.

Our apartment has *its* own entrance. (possessive)
The river overran *its* banks. (possessive)
BUT
It's so nice to see you again. (contraction of *it is*)
I hear that *it's* cold outside. (contraction of *it is*)

Directions: Substitute contractions for the words in parentheses wherever possible.

1. Curt (was not) able to find his umbrella.
2. Our plane (did not) take off on time.
3. (We are) sure that (it is) too early to go.
4. (There is) a student whom I (have not) met.
5. (Let us) help the bird that injured (its) wing.

SENTENCE EXERCISE

Directions: Rekey the following sentences in the spaces provided, indicating possession or contraction of the words in parentheses wherever necessary.

EXAMPLE:

(I am) sure that (there is) a pot of gold at the (rainbow) end.

I'm sure that there's a pot of gold at the rainbow's end.

1. (We are) sorry that Max is ill and (cannot) go to (Mickey) graduation.

_____

2. (Let us) wait backstage to get both (actress) autographs.

_____

3. (I am) going to invite (Bess) husband to go swimming with us.

_____

4. (There is) a different speaker each week at the honor (student) meeting.

_____

5. My (mother) friend works in the (children) department of the local store.

_____

6. I (do not) remember ever seeing a seal balance a ball on (its) nose.

_____

7. Each (man) wife was present at the annual dinner of the (men) basketball team.

_____

_____

8. If (it is) possible, I would like to go to the (Mendoza) barbeque.

_____

9. We freed the (fox) paw from the (trap) grip.

_____

10. It (would not) have been possible to care for all the (traveler) needs without two (stewardess) assistance.

_____

_____

DICTIONARY USAGE

Directions: Here are the more difficult words and their meanings that appear in the assignments in this unit. Study them carefully; complete the sentences that follow.

acclaim (noun)	applause, praise
challenge (noun and verb)	to invite to compete
coach (noun)	one who instructs or trains a team
debate (noun and verb)	to discuss a question by the presentation of arguments by both sides.
debut (noun)	a first public appearance
jitters (noun)	extreme nervousness
oceanfront	an area that faces the ocean
reaction	response
root (verb) to _____ for	to wish success or lend support to
sponsor (verb)	to pay the expense of an undertaking

Directions for completing the following sentences: Select the appropriate word from the above list, and key it in each blank.

1. The arguments presented by both sides during the _____ were interesting, but my team won.
2. The house is on the _____ and always has a delightful sea breeze.
3. The town cannot afford the parade, but a major corporation has agreed to _____ it.
4. My brother is making his _____ as an actor; I hope that he receives the critics' _____ .
5. His _____ to the accident was quick; he called the police.
6. The cheerleaders are supposed to _____ for their team.
7. The pirate _____ the captain to a duel.
8. The actress had opening-night _____ and wouldn't go on.
9. To express our thanks for helping to make us a winning team, we gave the _____ a gold watch.
10. After his important discovery, the scientist received much _____ .

Directions: Key this personal note in modified block style with open punctuation. You are to insert the following punctuation usages: 6 apostrophes indicating possession and 6 apostrophes indicating contraction.

Use a full sheet of paper.
Margins: 50-space line (elite 26-81; pica 17-72)
Tabs and center points: Elite 51; pica 42

Key the date at the center of the 15th line from the top edge of the paper. Quadruple-space, and key the salutation. Double-space after the salutation, and single-space the body. Double-space after the body; key the complimentary at the center point of the paper.

June 2, 19--

Dear Myron

This mornings announcement at the breakfast table
was a surprise. Our family will spend this years
vacation at the seashore. Well be going to Cape May
at the end of July, and were going to stay there for
two weeks. My parents announcement also included
the news that theyve already rented a house. Its
right on the oceanfront.

The seashore was my fathers choice. Last years
vacation was my two sisters choice, and we flew
to the West Coast.

Im looking forward to this vacation because I enjoy
swimming. Ill write to you when we arrive.

Sincerely

Directions: Key the following short report, indicating possessives and contractions wherever necessary. Refer to page 5 for a review of proofreader's marks.

Use a full sheet of paper.
Margins: 60-space line (elite 21-86; pica 12-77)
Tabs: Elite 26; pica 17
Center points: Elite 51; pica 42

Center the title on the 12th line from the top edge of the paper for elite and the 10th line for pica. Quadruple-space to the first paragraph. Double-space the report. Indent paragraphs 5 spaces.

NOTE: You will not be able to copy this report line for line. Use your judgment as to where each line should end within the margins given.

Center   My Acting Debut   *quadruple space*

Theres no business like show business. I was the star of the Drama Clubs produc-

tion, <u>Snow White and the Seven Dwarfs</u>. My brother Jess part was that of one

of the dwarfs. Three students reviewed it for our newspaper.   ¶   Just

before the opening I suddenly *stet* thought, "Todays rehearsal is the last one Before

tonights performance"; and I began to get opening-night jitters. well, the

audiences reaction was wonderful; and I received the critics acclaim. ¶ Ive

learned a lot about the theater; for example, an actors belief is that its bad

luck to whistle back stage. The theater is now a part of my life, and

Im on my way to becomeing a famous actress.

Directions: Key this personal note in block style with open punctuation, indicating possessives and contractions wherever necessary.

Use a full sheet of paper.
Margins: 50-space line (elite 26-81; pica 17-72)

All parts of the note are to be keyed at the left margin. Key the date on the 15th line from the top edge of the paper. Quadruple-space, and key the salutation. Double-space after the salutation, and single-space the body. Double-space after the body; key the complimentary close.

March 15, 19--

Dear Tony

Im on my schools debating team. We are the citys top debating team, and we have been challenged to debate New Orleans winning team.

Of course, we cant refuse such a challenge, and well be going there next month. In New Orleans our team will stay at the other team members homes.

We owe much of our success to Mr. Moss efforts. Mr. Moss is the teams coach as well as our English teacher.

The entire town is rooting for us. Gus Miller of Gus Sportswear is sponsoring our trip. The mayors wife will accompany us.

Ill tell you all about the debate when I see you.

Sincerely

CONTEXT CHECK

[What is the communication about?]

Directions: Following are 3 groups of sentences concerning the 2 letters and the report in this unit that you have keyed. Fill in the blanks, or indicate the correct answers as otherwise requested. You may refer to the communications.

HELPFUL-HINT LETTER

1. The writer and his/her family will spend their vacation at the _____ _____ .
2. They are going to _____ and will stay for _____ weeks.
3. This year's vacation choice was that of the writer's _____ .

YOU'RE ON YOUR OWN—ASSIGNMENT NO. 1

1. The writer starred in the Drama Club's production of _____ _____ .
2. The writer's brother also had a part in the play; he was one of the _____ .
3. Check the correct sentence:
   (   ) The critics liked the writer's performance.
   (   ) The critics did not like the writer's performance.

YOU'RE ON YOUR OWN—ASSIGNMENT NO. 2

1. The writer is on his/her school's _____ team.
2. The writer's team has been challenged to debate the top team in _ _____ .
3. Much of the team's success is owed to Mr. Moss, the team's _____ _____ .

PROOFREADING ASSIGNMENT

Directions: Insert proofreader's marks to indicate corrections in the following paragraph. Here are the 6 marks that will have to be inserted.

=	capitalize	let's buy it.	Let's buy it.
⌒	close up	ware house	warehouse
#	insert space	I am happy.	I am happy.
/	lowercase letter	Don't Go.	Don't go.
⊔	move left	Find the key. It's lost.	Find the key. It's lost.
∿	transpose	reciept	receipt

In my art class We are learning all abuot the artists of the

last century. I especially like paintings by Claude Monet,

which are realistic butnot like photographs. he liked to

paint out doors in natural light.

9 Troublesome Words

Performance Objective: Upon completion of this and the following unit, you will be able to apply the rules for correct usage of certain words in written communications.

9-1 BAD, BADLY

Bad — not good, wicked, sorry, ill. It is used after the verbs *feel* and *look*.

Badly — in a bad manner

> I feel bad because you are not well. (after verb *feel*)
> Harry looked bad after he ate the salad. (after verb *looked*)
> The children behaved badly today. (in a bad manner)

TRY-OUT EXERCISE

Directions: Rekey the following sentences, filling in the blanks with the proper usage of *bad* or *badly*.

1. I felt _____ when I heard the sad news.
2. Joan looks _____ since the accident.
3. My brother acted _____ after he lost the game.
4. Don't feel _____ because I forgot your birthday.
5. Some people behaved _____ during the assembly.

9-2 BESIDE, BESIDES

Beside — at the side of

Besides — in addition to:
          moreover, in addition

(Notice the use of commas in the second and third examples below.)

> Bruce sat beside Zeff at the game. (at the side of Zeff)
> Besides Bruce, Zeff and Lisa were also there. (in addition to Bruce)
> Besides, Bruce has extra tickets. (moreover)

TRY-OUT EXERCISE

Directions: Key the following sentences, filling in the blanks with the proper usage of *beside* or *besides*.

1. Who else passed the test _____ you?
2. I stood _____ Kelly during the ceremony.
3. It is too late to go; _____, it's snowing heavily.
4. The waitress placed the cup _____ the plate.
5. _____ you and Carmen, Janie has few friends.

9-3
BETTER, BEST

Better is used when comparing two items; *best* is used when there are more than two items.

> It would be better to wait than to walk in the rain.
> Help me choose the better of the two pictures.
> Her voice was judged the best in the citywide contest.

TRY-OUT EXERCISE

Directions: Rekey the following sentences, filling in the blanks with the proper usage of *better* or *best*.

1. It would be _____ to go on Saturday than on Sunday.
2. Chuck was voted the _____ speaker in his class.
3. Of the three workers, Daisy Cortes does the _____ job.
4. I read both stories but liked the shorter one _____ .
5. It's _____ to resign than to work under such conditions.

9-4
BETWEEN, AMONG

Between is used when referring to two persons or things; *among* is used when referring to more than two persons or things.

> Let's divide the cupcake between Marnie and Barney.
> Let's divide the pie among our six guests.

TRY-OUT EXERCISE

Directions: Rekey the following sentences, filling in the blanks with the proper usage of *between* or *among*.

1. Protests were heard _____ members of the losing team.
2. For dinner I had to decide _____ fish or meat.
3. The manager divided the work _____ two clerks.
4. Disagreement arose _____ four candidates in the race.
5. Josie chose a watch from _____ five styles.

9-5
LAY, LIE

Lay — to put or to place
Lie — to rest or recline

Lay is always followed by a direct object (a direct object answers the question *What*?). Each of the following sentences demonstrates the usage of *lay*. The action word or verb is underscored one time; the object of the verb is underscored twice.

Present: I lay the pencil on the desk.
            (What do I lay on the desk? Answer: the pencil)

Present
Participle: I am laying my coat over the chair.

Past: Jed laid the cards on the table.

Past
Participle: We have laid the plan before the committee.

Lie is never followed by a direct object.

Present: I <u>lie</u> down every day at four o'clock.

Present
Participle: Rona <u>is lying</u> down now.

Past: We <u>lay</u> down at four o'clock.

Past
Participle: Mary <u>has lain</u> in bed since yesterday.

PRINCIPAL PARTS OF LAY AND LIE

	Present	Present Participle	Past	Past Participle
LAY	lay	laying	laid	laid
LIE	lie	lying	lay	lain

HINT: When in doubt, mentally substitute the meaning of the word in place of the verb. The sentence will make sense only if the correct meaning is substituted.

I lay (put) the pencil on the desk.
I lie down (rest) every day at four o'clock.

TRY-OUT EXERCISE

Directions: Rekey the following sentences, filling in the blanks with the proper usage of *lay* or *lie*.

1. My dog _____ on the floor and plays with me.
2. He _____ his head on the pillow and slept.
3. I saw a penny _____ on the sidewalk.
4. Its mother has _____ the baby in the crib.
5. Last night I _____ down to sleep early.

SENTENCE EXERCISE

Directions: Rekey the following sentences in the spaces provided, selecting the correct word in parentheses.

EXAMPLE:

I felt so (bad, badly) after eating that I (laid, lay) down.

I felt so bad after eating that I lay down.

1. I knelt (beside, besides) all the puppies and chose one from (among, between) them.

_____

2. You look (bad, badly) since you began your diet; (beside, besides), you appear thinner.

_____

_____

3. Decide which of the two rings you like (better, best).

_____

4. I feel (bad, badly) because I couldn't settle the argument (among, between) Ray and Dan.

_____

5. (Beside, Besides) Harold, Carol volunteered for the job; it is (better, best) to have two people doing it than just one.

_____

_____

6. The child is behaving (bad, badly); he has not (laid, lain) down for his nap.

_____

7. Of all these ties, which is the (better, best) one for this shirt?

_____

8. I (laid, lay) the scarf (beside, besides) my new coat to match the color.

_____

9. The poor man has (lain, laid) there without assistance for ten minutes.

_____

10. (Beside, Besides) milk, the hostess served soda.

_____

DICTIONARY USAGE

Directions: Here are the more difficult words and their meanings that appear in the assignments in this unit. Study them carefully; complete the sentences that follow.

adopt	to take in as one's own
chores	regular tasks or jobs in a household
consider	to think about
deprived (verb)	to be without
forlornly	abandoned, miserably, hopelessly
huge	very large
recuperate	to get back to health; recover
select (verb)	to choose
stray (noun)	a homeless or lost cat or dog

Directions for completing the following sentences: Select the appropriate word from the above list, and key it in each blank.

1. The building is _____; it has 100 stories.
2. Mr. and Mrs. Jay have four children and want to _____ an orphan.
3. I will _____ going to college when I graduate.
4. Washing the dishes is one of my daily _____.
5. The nice lady loves animals and feeds every _____ she sees.
6. My doctor says it will take a week to _____ from the flu.
7. Here are five pens; _____ the one you want.
8. The homeless dog stood _____ in the snow waiting for someone to _____ it.
9. In some undemocratic countries, people are _____ of their rights.
10. My brother will _____ all the jobs offered to him, and he will _____ one.

Directions: Key this personal note in block style with open punctuation. Correct the 6 troublesome words that are not used properly.

Use a full sheet of paper.
Margins: 50-space line (elite 26-81; pica 17-72)

All parts of the note are to be keyed at the left margin. Key the date on the 15th line from the top edge of the paper. Quadruple-space, and key the salutation. Double-space after the salutation, and single-space the body. Double-space after the body; key the complimentary close.

January 15, 19--

Dear Bobbie

Please forgive me for not writing sooner, but I have
been very busy. Beside working hard in school, I am
helping my aunt.

As you know, between all my aunts I like Aunt Shirley
better. I feel so badly because she fell on the ice
and broke her arm. Since she lives alone, she decided
to stay with us while she recuperates.

Fortunately, Aunt Shirley laid in bed for just one day.
However, her arm will have to remain in a cast for
several more weeks. I am glad that she decided to
stay with us. We can help her; beside, she is fun to
be with.

Perhaps we can meet soon.

Sincerely

Directions: Key this personal note in modified block style with open punctuation. Correct any troublesome words that are not used properly.

Use a full sheet of paper.
Margins: 50-space line (elite 26-81; pica 17-72)
Tabs and center point: Elite 51; pica 42

Key the date at the center of the 15th line from the top edge of the paper. Quadruple-space, and key the salutation. Double-space after the salutation, and single-space the body. Double-space after the body; key the complimentary close at the center point of the paper.

NOTE: You will not be able to copy this note line for line. Use your judgment as to where each line should end within the margins given.

February 10, 19--

Dear Uncle David
¶ School was closed here today because of heavy snow. I did not feel too badly about it. I lay my books aside and prepared to go out in the snow.
¶ I was looking forward to building a huge snowman besides the garage. My mother, however, thought it would be best for me to take care of chores rather than play; beside, someone had to shovel the snow. If I had to choose between all my chores, shoveling the snow would be my last choice.
¶ Uncle David, I will be glad to go back to school tomorrow.
Sincerely

Directions: Key the following short report, correcting any troublesome words that are not used properly.

Use a full sheet of paper.
Margins: 60-space line (elite 21-86; pica 12-77)
Tabs: Elite 26; pica 17
Center points: Elite 51; pica 42

Center the title (KEY IN ALL CAPITAL LETTERS) on the 12th line from the top edge of the paper for elite and 10th line for pica. Quadruple-space to the first paragraph. Double-space the report. Indent paragraphs 5 spaces.

POOPSIE

     I have a black and white cat named Poopsie. She was treated bad when she was very young; she was a stray.

     Some people select their pets from between many cute, cuddly animals. I saw Poopsie standing forlornly by herself in the street with no other cats besides her, and I knew immediately that she was meant for me.

     Poopsie lays next to me all the time. She loves to eat and is making up for when she was deprived of food. Of the many foods I feed her, she likes "people" tuna fish better.

     If you want a pet, you should consider adopting a cat. Beside being easy to care for, they are extremely affectionate animals.

CONTEXT CHECK

[What is the
communication about?]

Directions: Following are three groups of sentences concerning the two letters and the report in this unit that you have keyed. Fill in the blanks, or indicate the correct answer as otherwise requested. You may refer to the communications.

HELPFUL-HINT LETTER

1. Aunt Shirley fell on the ice and _____ .
2. She is staying with the writer's family while she _____
   _____ .

3. Check whether the following sentence is true (   ) or false (   ):
   Aunt Shirley is not the writer's favorite aunt.

YOU'RE ON YOUR OWN—ASSIGNMENT NO. 1

1. The writer's school was closed because of _____ .
2. The writer was looking forward to building _____ .
3. Instead, the writer had to _____ .

YOU'RE ON YOUR OWN—ASSIGNMENT NO. 2

1. Poopsie was not treated well when she was very young; in fact, she
   was a _____ .
2. Poopsie's favorite food is _____ .
3. Cats are easy to care for, and they are _____ .

PROOFREADING ASSIGNMENT

Directions: Insert proofreader's marks to indicate corrections in the following paragraph. Here are the 6 marks that will have to be inserted.

≡	capitalize	Ask jane.	Ask Jane.
◯	close up	with out	without
⸔	delete	markked	marked
∧	insert	faling	falling
# ∧	insert space	Let's doit.	Let's do it.
⊙	insert period	Let's go	Let's go.

Tornadoes (or "twisters") cause muh damage. Windsas high as 230 miles an hour have been recorded during a tor nado. You can actually see a tornado it is a funnel-shaped cloud that reaches down from the skys to the ground.

NAME_____

SENTENCE REVIEW   *Directions:*   Rekey the following sentences in the spaces provided, inserting colons, semicolons, and commas; indicate possessives and contractions; correct any troublesome words.

EXAMPLE:

My uncles invitation didnt arrive therefore he wasnt present.

My uncle's invitation didn't arrive; therefore, he wasn't present.

1. The childrens teacher is arriving at 6 30 Ill wait for her.

_____

2. I received six gifts but the nicest one was from Mr. Chin, my fathers friend.

_____

3. Im not accepting my two cousins lunch invitation for the following reasons its raining, I have
no umbrella, and I have a cold.

_____

_____

4. Max felt bad and laid down beside he had nothing else to do.

_____

5. On his way to school, Bills brother slipped and he hurt his shoulder.

_____

6. Darin, make up your mind or you will lose your turn.

_____

7. Lets take the 12 06 train to the Smiths house.

_____

8. The mens bowling team meets on Fridays unfortunately this weeks meeting is cancelled.

_____

_____

9. The best man won the prize fight his fan clubs membership was delighted.

_____

_____

10. I feel badly because I lost the scarf that Frances mother gave me.

_____

11. The following people were at todays meeting Pat, Felix, Marta, and Deb.

_____

12. At the suggestion of the students teacher, they lay their picnic baskets on the grass besides the lake.

_____

_____

13. Cheryl behaved bad during the lecture she read a book.

_____

14. The ladies husbands waited patiently during their wives art class.

_____

15. Jay had to choose a watch from between all those lying in the showcase however he couldn't decide which he liked better.

_____

_____

Directions: Key the following short report. Use a full sheet of paper with a 60-space line; double-space the report. Wherever necessary, insert colons, semicolons, and commas; indicate possessives and contractions; correct any troublesome words that are not used properly.

MY VISIT TO THE ZOO

During the summer my best friends parents took us to the zoo. Following are some of the animals we saw zebras, lions, monkeys, giraffes, and deer.

Our days visit began at 10 30. I had never seen a zebra before I couldnt believe my eyes. Their black stripes look like an artists work. We threw fish to the seals and a cute, cuddly deer ate from my hand.

We sighted the giraffes heads from the distance of course their long necks make them so tall. We saw a lion cub laying besides its mother, a huge lioness and an elephants long trunk daintily took the peanuts we fed it.

We left the zoo at 4 45 in my opinion it was a great day.

Directions: Key this personal note in block style with open punctuation. Use a full sheet of paper with a 60-space line. Wherever necessary, insert colons, semicolons, and commas; indicate possessives and contractions; correct any troublesome words that are not used properly.

June 5, 19--

Dear Xavier

My brother Les bought a new car after choosing carefully between three models. He was anxious to show it off therefore he asked me to take a drive with him. I was eager to ride in Les car and met him at 9 00 the next morning.

Les thought it would be best to drive in the country rather than stay in town. We drove for several hours and we stopped to have a picnic lunch of cold chicken, turkey, and ham. We got into the car to continue on our way it wouldnt start.

I looked at my brothers face needless to say I felt so badly for him. His face had a sad, hopeless expression but it soon changed. The cars trouble was minor, and he is now very happy with it.

See you soon.

Sincerely

Directions: Insert proofreader's marks to indicate corrections in the following paragraph. Here are the 6 marks that will have to be inserted.

≡	capitalize	Where's janie?	Where's Janie?
⸿	delete	It's snowwing.	It's snowing.
∧	insert	Hw are you?	How are you?
#	insert space	I'mfine	I'm fine.
/	lowercase letter	It's Raining.	It's raining.
∿	transpose	How are yuo?	How are you?

Elephant herds are dwindling because of man's desire for Ivory.
it's treu that ivory is very lovely;however, it's so sad to
see pictures of elephant that have been killed just for their
ivorry tusks.

10 Troublesome Words (Continued)

Performance Objective:

Upon completion of this unit, you will be able to apply the rules for correct usage of certain words in written communications.

10-1
FEWER, LESS

Fewer — used with nouns that can be counted

(HINT: *fewer* precedes a plural noun)

Less — used with nouns that cannot be counted

There are fewer students in class today.
I want less sugar in my tea.

TRY-OUT EXERCISE

Directions: Rekey the following sentences, filling in the blanks with the proper usage of *few* or *less*.

1. _____ members than usual attended the meeting.
2. I must spend _____ time at practice today.
3. Edna made _____ mistakes on this test than the last one.
4. Each year _____ people march in the parade.
5. The rain caused _____ damage than expected.

10-2
LEAVE, LET

Leave — to go away or depart
Let — to allow or permit

I must leave my house shortly.
Let me open the door for you.

TRY-OUT EXERCISE

Directions: Rekey the following sentences, filling in the blanks with the proper usage of *leave* or *let*.

1. _____ Dennis help you do it.
2. Our plane will _____ at midnight.
3. The nurse would not _____ me disturb you.
4. I won't _____ Ken borrow my bicycle.
5. Don't _____ anyone take my place in line.

10-3
PASSED, PAST

Passed — moved by; undergone successfully
Past — gone by in time

Jake waved as he passed us. (moved by)
I passed all my final exams. (underwent successfully)
My grandmother tells stories about the past. (gone by in time)
It rained all this past week. (gone by in time)

Directions: Rekey the following sentences, filling in the blanks with the proper usage of *passed* or *past*.

1. The bus _____ us without stopping.
2. During the _____ six months, I was absent once.
3. Gina _____ me in the hallway.
4. The old woman is living in the _____.
5. This _____ month I learned that I _____ my history test.

10-4
RAISE, RISE

Raise — to lift something; to increase in size or amount.
Rise — to get up, move up, or ascend

Principal parts of RAISE and RISE

	Present	Present Participle	Past	Past Participle
RAISE	raise	raising	raised	raised
RISE	rise	rising	rose	risen

HINT: *Raise* is always followed by a direct object (a direct object answers the question "What?").

Raise the window.
(Raise what? Answer: the window)
BUT
The sun will rise at 6:00 a.m. today.

Note that the past tense of *rise* is *rose*: The temperature rose to 80 degrees.

Directions: Rekey the following sentences, filling in the blanks with the proper usage of *raise* or *rise*.

1. If you agree, please _____ your hand.
2. Her boss will _____ Judy's salary.
3. This morning I _____ my head from the pillow as the sun _____ .
4. The heat will soon _____ and warm the house.
5. The treasure hunters have _____ the sunken ship.

10-5
REAL, VERY

Real — genuine
Very — the extreme (to a high or low degree); exceedingly

HINT: *real* describes a noun (person, place, or thing)
very usually modifies an adjective (descriptive word)

The ring contains a real diamond.
real describes the noun *diamond*

The ring contains a very large diamond.
very modifies the adjective *large*

TRY-OUT EXERCISE

Directions: Rekey the following sentences, filling in the blanks with the proper usage of *real* or *very*.

1. Kate was _____ late for an important date.
2. I am saving for a jacket made of _____ fur.
3. The room looks _____ empty without a table.
4. I felt _____ bad after losing my ring with the _____ ruby.
5. Jeff is _____ excited about receiving the award.

10-6
SURE, SURELY

Sure — certain or positive
Surely — certainly

HINT: *certain* can be mentally substituted for *sure*
          certainly can be mentally substituted for *surely*

I am sure that you will recover soon. (certain)
Surely you will recover soon. (certainly)

TRY-OUT EXERCISE

Directions: Rekey the following sentences, filling in the blanks with the proper usage of *sure* or *surely*.

1. After all that work, Tony should _____ pass.
2. I am _____ that your efforts will be rewarded.
3. Please be _____ to turn out the light.
4. _____ we can understand Tim's point of view.
5. The rain will _____ stop shortly.

10-7
TO, AT, BY

These words are prepositions implying various movements:

To — the movement is toward a person, place, or thing
At — the movement has already occurred, and you are there
By — the movement is one of passing

I am going to Phil's home. (you are going toward his home)
I am at Phil's home. (you are at his home)
I am going by Phil's home on my way to the beach. (you are going past his home)

TRY-OUT EXERCISE

Directions: Rekey the following sentences, filling in the blanks with the proper usage of *to*, *at*, or *by*.

1. The singer sat _____ the pianist's side.
2. We drove _____ the accident on our way here.
3. Come _____ my house for dinner tonight.
4. Please stop _____ the florist for some roses.
5. Meet me _____ the fountain in the park.

SENTENCE EXERCISE

Directions: Rekey the following sentences in the spaces provided, selecting the correct word in parentheses.

EXAMPLE:

I have (fewer, less) pairs of shoes than she.

I have fewer pairs of shoes than she.

1. If the landlord (raises, rises) our rent, we (sure, surely) will be angry.

_____

2. As I walked (to, at, by) Jess's house, I waved and continued on my way.

_____

3. (Fewer, Less) people were in the graduating class this (passed, past) year.

_____

4. My parents were (real, very) annoyed with me for staying out late; they refused to (leave, let) me go to the game today.

_____

_____

5. The sun (raised, rose) at 6:40 this morning.

_____

6. I was (real, very) disappointed because I received (fewer, less) Christmas gifts this year.

_____

_____

7. Nicky was (sure, surely) walking fast as he (passed, past) me in the hall.

_____

8. You have (fewer, less) chance of catching cold if you don't (leave, let) your feet get wet.

_____

_____

9. (Sure, Surely) you can (leave, let) me know if the books were ordered.

_____

10. I stopped (to, at, by) the dean's office to find out if I had (passed, past) my exams.

_____

_____

DICTIONARY USAGE

Directions: Here are the more difficult words and their meanings that appear in the assignments in this unit. Study them carefully; complete the sentences that follow.

benefit (noun)	a performance to raise funds for some persons or cause.
claim (verb)	to take possession as the rightful owner
docilely	easily taught, led, or managed; obediently
hypnotize	to put into an artificial sleep under which one loses willpower and is open to suggestion
intention	a determination to act in a certain way
reinforce	to strengthen with additional force or material
reserve (verb)	to have something set aside or held for special use
support (noun)	that which holds up someone or something
visible	in full view or readily seen

Directions for completing the following sentences: Select the appropriate word from the above list, and key it in each blank.

1. The teacher explained the new lesson and then placed two examples on the board to _____ her explanation.
2. The thread was so fine that the stitches were not _____.
3. My scarf was found in Ms. Bell's classroom, and I went there to _____ it.
4. I hope that we can _____ seats for the play; it may be sold out.
5. Dr. Clark will _____ Ruth and, while she is sleeping, suggest that she stop smoking.
6. The dog bit Clem but then walked _____ to its owner and licked his hand.
7. There will be a _____ to raise funds for the flood victims.
8. We have no _____ of going there today because it's raining.
9. The old man is weak and uses a cane for _____.
10. Stitch the seam twice to _____ it.

HELPFUL-HINT LETTER

Directions: Key this personal note in modified block style with open punctuation. Correct the nine troublesome words that are not used properly.

Use a full sheet of paper.
Margins: 50-space line (elite 26-81; pica 17-72)
Tabs and center points: Elite 51; pica 42

Key the date at the center of the 15th line from the top edge of the paper. Quadruple-space, and key the salutation. Double-space after the salutation, and single-space the body. Double-space after the body; key the complimentary close at the center point of the paper.

                                        December 4, 19--

Dear Nancy

As I was walking to school the other day, I was real
surprised to see a bracelet lying on the ground. I
sure had no intention of keeping it, but I did not
know how to find its owner.

My parents agreed to leave me place an ad in the newspaper. Three days past, and the phone rang. As I
rised the receiver to my ear, I just knew that the
owner of the bracelet was calling. It was the lady
who had lost the bracelet.

The lady agreed to come by our house and claim the
bracelet. My parents would not leave me accept the
reward she offered, but I sure felt real proud to
have done such a good deed.

                        Sincerely

Directions: Key the following short report, correcting any troublesome words that are not used properly. Refer to page 5 for a review of proofreader's marks.

Use a full sheet of paper.
Margins: 60-space line (elite 21-86; pica 12-77)
Tabs: Elite 26; pica 17
Center points: Elite 51; pica 42

Center the title on the 12th line from the top edge of the paper for elite and the 10th line for pica. Quadruple-space to the first paragraph. Double-space the report. Indent paragraphs 5 spaces.

NOTE: You will not be able to copy this report line for line. Use your judgment as to where each line should end within the margins given.

quadruple space

Center

My First Visit to a Circus

Because I past all my final exams, my family decided to celebrate by

going to a Circus. We all loved it. We saw an elephant dance.

Then her trainer lay on the ground; the elephants past over him without

touching him. we saw a magician hypnotize his assistant; her body then

rised in the air at his direction with no visible means of support. Normally,

lions do not leave humans come near them. At the circus, no less than six

lions ~~docilely~~ *stet* obeyed their trainer's commands. Of course, he did rise his

whip to re inforce his words. I intend to go by the circus each

yaer when it returns to town. It is surely great entertainment.

Directions: Key this personal-business letter in modified block style with indented paragraphs and open punctuation. Correct any troublesome words that are not used properly.

Use a full sheet of paper.
Margins: 50-space line (elite 26-81; pica 17-72)
Tabs: Elite 31, 51; pica 22, 42
Center points: Elite 51; pica 42

Key your return address at the center of the 13th line from the top edge of the paper; the date is on line 15 under your two-line return address. Quadruple-space after the date, and key the inside address (name and address of person to whom the letter is going). Double-space; key the salutation. Double-space after the salutation, and single-space the body. Double-space after the body; key the complimentary close at the center point. Quadruple-space, and key your name at the center point.

Your street address
Your city, state ZIP
November 15, 19--

Mr. Gordon Herman
Ticket Sales
Palace Theater
1025 Ascot Street
Hackensack, NY 07601-1675

Dear Mr. Herman

This passed week my brother and I read in the newspaper that there will be a benefit by the rock group, the Ripples, to rise money for hungry children throughout the world. We would be real unhappy if we missed their only performance in this city.

Since the box office is not yet open, we would like to order tickets by mail. We surely hope that you will leave us reserve ten seats; however, if you are limiting the number, we would like no less than five. When the box office opens, I will go by the theater to pick them up.

We are sure looking forward to seeing the Ripples in person.

Sincerely

Your name

CONTEXT CHECK

[What is the communication about?]

Directions: Following are three groups of sentences concerning the two letters and the report in this unit that you have keyed. Fill in the blanks; you may refer to the communications.

HELPFUL-HINT LETTER

1. The writer found a _____ lying on the ground.
2. In order to find the owner of the object, the writer placed _____
   _____ .

3. Upon claiming the object found by the writer, the owner offered a
   _____ .

YOU'RE ON YOUR OWN — ASSIGNMENT NO. 1

1. Two kinds of animals the writer saw perform at the circus were
   the _____ and the _____ .
2. After the magician hypnotized his assistant, her body _____
   _____ .

3. The lion trainer reinforced his commands by using a _____
   _____ .

YOU'RE ON YOUR OWN — ASSIGNMENT NO. 2

1. The name of the group giving the benefit performance is _____
   _____ .

2. The money raised from this performance wil be used to help feed
   _____ .

3. The writer and his brother would like to order a minimum of ____
   _____ tickets.

PROOFREADING ASSIGNMENT

Directions: Insert proofreader's marks to indicate corrections in the following paragraph. Here are the 6 marks that will have to be inserted.

≡	capitalize	i see him.	I see him.
⌒	close up	We can not go.	We cannot go.
ꝗ	delete	Let's have dinnner.	Let's have dinner.
⋀	insert	Jean is nt well.	Jean is not well.
⊙	insert period	I love ice cream I prefer vanilla.	I love ice cream. I prefer vanilla.
/	lowercase	You Must come.	You must come.

My sister susie and I flew to Califrnia last summer to

visit our cousins They live in San Francisco. Susie and

I had a wonderfull time. Taking a ride on a cable car was

the high light of our entire Trip.

11 Numbers

Performance Objective: Upon completion of this unit, you will be able to apply the rules for spelling out numbers and expressing them in figures in written communications.

11-1
NUMBERS FROM ONE THROUGH TEN AND ABOVE

Numbers from one through ten are generally spelled out; numbers above ten are expressed in figures.

> I bought two lamps for my room.
> The building has 27 floors.

TRY-OUT EXERCISE

Directions: Rekey the following sentences, expressing the numbers correctly.

1. Please water the 6 flower pots.
2. Mary Ann bought 10 apples and 4 bananas.
3. We spent 17 days in London this past summer.
4. There are nine people waiting for the shop to open.
5. My school is only eleven minutes from my home.

11-2
INDEFINITE AMOUNTS

Indefinite or approximate amounts are spelled out.

In each of the following examples, the underscored words tell the reader that the amounts that follow are not exact.

> I read <u>about</u> fifteen pages and fell asleep.
> <u>Approximately</u> one hundred guests were at the wedding.
> The waiting list contains <u>at least</u> twenty names. (no fewer than twenty, not necessarily twenty)

TRY-OUT EXERCISE

Directions: Rekey the following sentences, expressing the numbers correctly.

1. The restaurant has approximately 20 tables.
2. Drive about 200 feet, and turn left at the light.
3. The test contained at least 18 short-answer questions.
4. Fewer than 30 people signed up for the class.
5. Almost seven minutes are left to finish the test.

11-3
A NUMBER AT THE BEGINNING OF A SENTENCE

Numbers that begin a sentence are spelled out.

> Nineteen tourists were on the bus.
> Thirty-five boys tried out for the team.
> Eighty-four students were in the graduating class.
> Three hundred people boarded the jumbo jet.

Note the hyphen between spelled-out numbers such as *thirty-five* and *eighty-four*.

TRY-OUT EXERCISE

Directions: Rekey the following sentences, expressing the numbers correctly.

1. 500 jelly beans are in the jar.
2. One marcher left the parade early.
3. 23 subscriptions were sold by Ben in one week.
4. Twelve slices of bread are in the package.
5. 80 people were injured during the tornado.

11-4
DATES

When the day appears after the month, use figures to express it.

> My birthday is on March 23.
> September 5 is the first day of school.

When the day appears alone or before the month, use figures plus *d*, *th*, or *st*.

> My birthday is on the 23d of March.
> The 5th of September is the first day of school.
> Let's meet on the 21st instead of the 22d.

TRY-OUT EXERCISE

Directions: Rekey the following sentences, expressing the numbers correctly.

1. I have a dentist's appointment on September 13th.
2. Income taxes are due by the 15 of April.
3. Can you be here on June 17 instead of the 21?
4. Jim's vacation began on the 3d of August and ended on August 10th.
5. We will arrive on December 31st.

11-5
MONEY

Exact amounts of money are expressed in figures. When there are just dollars and no cents, omit the decimal point and the two zeros.

> Your share of the bill is $9.75.
> The clerk charged me $4 too much.
> The fur jacket costs $200. (There is a period at the end of the sentence, not a decimal.)

TRY-OUT EXERCISE

Directions: Rekey the following sentences, expressing the numbers correctly.

1. Margo won $50.00 in the raffle.
2. Each student contributed 1 dollar toward the gift.
3. The scarf that I lost cost eight dollars.
4. Ned needs eighteen dollars and 50 cents to pay for his uniform.
5. I am returning $3.00 and owe $12.00.

SENTENCE EXERCISE

Directions: Rekey the following sentences in the spaces provided, expressing the numbers correctly. If a sentence requires no change, key *correct* in the space below it.

EXAMPLE:

Each of the 4 books I bought was reduced to $2.00.

Each of the four books I bought was reduced to $2.

1. 200 signatures are on the petition, but about 50 more are needed.

_____

2. Golda knitted 2 sweaters, 3 hats, and one blanket for the baby.

_____

3. A deposit of $20.00 is required by October 1st if you are going on the trip.

_____

4. At least 15 people were in the competition besides me, but I won the prize of one hundred dollars.

_____

_____

5. Our dog Poochie gave birth to four puppies on June 12.

_____

6. Each of the thirty students in the class contributed 3 dollars toward the gift.

_____

7. About 25 fans were waiting at the stage door for the 9 cast members.

_____

8. On the 22 of September, 18 club members voted to increase the dues.

_____

9. Jeremy has a collection of seventy-five old comic books, and one is worth two hundred and sixty dollars.

_____

_____

10. 3 of my friends flew to Miami on the 31st of July and returned on August 3d.

_____

DICTIONARY USAGE

Directions: Here are the more difficult words and their meanings that appear in the assignments in this unit. Study them carefully; complete the sentences that follow.

compile	to make up, put together
confide (to _____ in)	to share a secret with
credit (noun and verb)	to enter a payment in an account
indicate	to point out, direct attention to
issue (verb)	to send or give out
pamper	to coddle, spoil, treat with excessive attention
pool (noun)	a fund made up of contributions from a number of people
superb	excellent

Directions for completing the following sentences: Select the appropriate word from the above list, and key it in each blank.

1. Return the watch you don't want, and the store will _____ your account.
2. The light over the door _____ to the nurse that the patient needs help.
3. Clara _____ a list of gifts she wants for Christmas and mailed it to Santa.
4. The salesperson will _____ a credit slip to the customer upon the return of the merchandise.
5. Gelsey is a spoiled child because her parents _____ her.
6. I will _____ in you because I trust you.
7. Renoir was a _____ painter whose work is constantly admired.
8. The ship's _____ was won by the passenger who most closely guessed the number of miles traveled that day.
9. Please _____ your preference by placing a check mark next to it.
10. We always eat at this restaurant because the food is _____ .

Directions: Key this personal-business letter in block style with open punctuation, expressing the numbers correctly. It contains the following usages of numbers: three numbers that are to be spelled out, one number that is to be expressed in figures, one date, and three expressions of dollars and cents.

Use a full sheet of paper.
Margins: 50-space line (elite 26-81; pica 17-72)

All parts of the letter are to be keyed at the left margin. Key your return address on the 13th line from the top edge of the paper; the date is on line 15 under your two-line return address. Quadruple-space after the date, and key the inside address (name and address of person to whom the letter is going). Double-space; key the salutation. Double-space after the salutation, and single-space the body. Double-space after the body; key the complimentary close. Quadruple-space, and key your name.

NOTE: You will not be able to copy this letter exactly as it appears. Use your judgment as to where each line should end within the margins given.

Your street address
Your city, state ZIP
December 5, 19--

LaMode Specialty Stores
1351 Castle Hill Drive
Minneapolis, MN 55430-9215

Ladies and Gentlemen

About 10 days ago, I purchased 3 scarves. However,
I kept 1 and returned the others.

The scarves had been charged to my mother's account.
Those that I returned on November 27th were credited
to that account. My mother's monthly statement in-
dicates that credit was issued for nine dollars
instead of $10.00. As you will see from your records,
each scarf was $5.00.

My mother would like to pay within the thirty-day
payment period but is waiting for the correction to
be made.

Cordially

Your name

Directions: Key this personal note in modified block style with open punctuation, expressing the numbers correctly.

Use a full sheet of paper.
Margins: 50-space line (elite 26-81; pica 17-72)
Tabs and center points: Elite 51; pica 42

Key the date at the center of the 15th line from the top edge of the paper. Quadruple-space, and key the salutation. Double-space after the salutation, and single-space the body. Double-space after the body; key the complimentary close at the center point of the paper.

NOTE: You will not be able to copy this letter exactly as it appears. Use your judgment as to where each line should end within the margins given.

September 15, 19--

Dear Gwen

¶ On October 22d I am having a birthday party, and I am now compiling my guest list. ¶ 50 names were on my first list. However, I have narrowed the list to twenty-five of my best friends.

¶ The party will take place at Walter's Water Wheel, which is about 12 minutes from the center of town. A 3-piece band will provide music for dancing.

¶ Please plan to help me celebrate my birthday on the 22 of October. You will receive an invitation soon.

Sincerely

P.S. I did not forget about the six dollars you loaned me. I will return it when I see you.

Directions: Key the following short report, expressing the numbers correctly.

Use a full sheet of paper.
Margins: 60-space line (elite 21-86; pica 12-77)
Tabs: Elite 26; pica 17
Center points: Elite 51; pica 42

Center the title (KEY IN ALL CAPITAL LETTERS) on line 12 from the top edge of the paper for elite and line 10 for pica. Quadruple-space to the first paragraph. Double-space the report. Indent paragraphs 5 spaces.

NOTE: You will not be able to copy this report exactly as it appears. Use your judgment as to where each line should end within the margins given.

MY FIRST AIRPLANE RIDE

My first ride in an airplane was on the 23 of December when my parents and I flew to California for 10 days.

As soon as the plane lifted off the ground, we were pampered by 3 flight attendants. After we were in the air for about 20 minutes, a superb lunch was served. 15 minutes after lunch, we saw a terrific movie.

The people around us were so nice. An elderly gentleman confided in us that he had flown ninety times. Toward the trip's end, 9 of the other passengers and my father each put $1.00 into a pool; the person who came closest to guessing the exact time we touched ground won the ten dollars. It was my father.

I was having such a good time that I was sorry to land.

CONTEXT CHECK

[What is the
communication about?]

Directions: Following are three groups of sentences concerning the two letters and the report in this unit that you have keyed. Fill in the blanks, or indicate the correct answers as otherwise requested. You may refer to the communications.

HELPFUL-HINT LETTER

1. How many scarves did the writer purchase? _____
   How many scarves did the writer return? _____
2. The price of each scarf was _____ .
3. When the writer returned the scarves, credit was issued in the amount of _____ instead of _____ .

YOU'RE ON YOUR OWN—ASSIGNMENT NO. 1

1. The date of the writer's birthday party is _____ .
2. The party will take place at the restaurant called _____
   _____ .
3. How many of the writer's friends will attend? _____

YOU'RE ON YOUR OWN—ASSIGNMENT NO. 2

1. On December 23 the writer flew to _____ .
2. In your opinion, was the writer treated well on board the plane?
   (check one)   Yes _____   No _____
3. At the end of the trip, who came closest to guessing the exact time the plane touched ground? _____

PROOFREADING ASSIGNMENT

Directions: Insert proofreader's marks to indicate corrections in the following paragraph. Here are the 6 marks that will have to be inserted.

≡	capitalize	Is ida here?	Is Ida here?
⊂	close up	Go with out me.	Go without me.
∧	insert	It's raning.	It's raining.
/	lowercase letter	Let's Go.	Let's go.
⊏	move left	It's eight o'clock. You're late.	It's eight o'clock. You're late.
∿	transpose	handkercheif	handkerchief

My sister Cheryl attends a col lege in another state.
She would like to become an elementry school Teacher like
our mother. cheryl probably will go on to graduate school
and then come home to taech in this city.

12 Quotation Marks

Performance Objective:

Upon completion of this unit, you will be able to apply the rules for quotation marks in business communications; you will be able to apply the rules for indicating titles of publications and sections within publications.

12-1
WITH DIRECT QUOTATIONS

A direct quotation is a person's exact words; enclose direct quotations in quotation marks. An indirect quotation, or paraphrase, is a rearrangement of a person's exact words; quotation marks are not used with indirect quotations.

Direct quotation: My dentist said, "Be sure that you remember to cut down on your intake of sweets in order to avoid so many cavities."

Indirect quotation or paraphrase: My dentist told me that, in order to get fewer cavities, I should stop eating so many sweets.

Here are additional examples of direct quotations:

Blanche said, "I can't meet you today."
The sign reads, "Please keep off the grass."
Jules warned, "Don't tease the dog."

Note that in each quotation a comma is placed after the verb or action word (*said*, *reads*, *warned*), and the first word of the quotation is capitalized. In addition, the period at the end of each sentence is inside the quotation mark.

TRY-OUT EXERCISE

Directions: Rekey the following sentences, placing quotation marks around direct quotations. Use the proper punctuation for direct quotations.

1. Shelly said here are some magazines that you might like.
2. Upon receiving the roses, our hostess told us that they were her favorite flower.
3. The travel poster reads visit Paris in the spring.
4. My doctor told me to lose some weight.
5. The bus driver replied yes, I stop at Main Street.

12-2
WITH COMMAS

Commas are placed within quotation marks. Notice in the following examples that the comma separates each quotation from the words that follow.

"I can't meet you today," said Blanche.
"Please keep off the grass," reads the sign.
"Don't tease the dog," Jules warned.

TRY-OUT EXERCISE

Directions: Rekey the following sentences, inserting quotation marks in their proper positions.

1. There is a limit to my patience, I told the clerk.
2. Your answer is correct, said the teacher.
3. I will haunt this house forever, whispered the ghost.
4. No, I am not at all well, answered Adele.
5. No smoking allowed, warned the policeman.

12-3
WITH COLONS AND SEMICOLONS

Colons and semicolons are placed outside quotation marks.

The lawyer said, "My client is innocent"; and the jury agreed.*
Two people heard Jeff murmur, "I am going home": Milly and Bill.
(Note the two spaces after the colon.)

(*See Unit 7, item 7-2, for rule on semicolon between independent clauses.)

TRY-OUT EXERCISE

Directions: Rekey the following sentences, inserting quotation marks in their proper positions; capitalize wherever necessary.

1. Rosie replied, I didn't take it; but she lied.
2. Two people answered the ad that read, part-time clerk needed: Cal and Hal.
3. Dina said, I won't forget to buy the cake; and she didn't.
4. Arlene suggested, let's take a taxi; but we didn't have enough money.
5. I still had two chores to finish when my mother said, go to bed: sweep the porch and walk the dog.

12-4
WITH QUESTION MARKS AND EXCLAMATION POINTS

Question marks and exclamation points may be placed either inside or outside quotation marks, depending upon the meaning of the sentence.

If a question is being quoted, the question mark is placed inside the quotation marks.

The teacher asked, "Have you finished?"

If a statement is being quoted, the question mark is placed outside the quotation marks.

Did you hear your teacher say, "Finish the test"? (The question is not part of the quotation.)

If an exclamation is being quoted, the exclamation point is placed inside the quotation marks.

> The auctioneer shouted, "Sold to the highest bidder!"

If a statement is being quoted, the exclamation point is placed outside the quotation marks.

> Stop repeating, "I'm sorry I came"! (The exclamation is not part of the quotation.)

TRY-OUT EXERCISE

Directions: Rekey the following sentences, inserting quotation marks in their proper positions; capitalize wherever necessary.

1. Jim asked, can you help me this afternoon?
2. The sign reads, absolute silence in this room!
3. Didn't you hear me say, be sure to close the door?
4. The umpire shouted, it's a home run!
5. The butcher asked, how many pounds of meat do you want?

12-5
WITH PUBLICATIONS

Chapters of books and titles of articles in magazines and newspapers are enclosed in quotation marks, and their most important words are capitalized.* Titles of books, magazines, and newspapers are typed in ALL CAPITAL LETTERS or are underscored; when they are underscored the most important words are capitalized.*

*Do not capitalize articles (*a, an, the*) or short prepositions and conjunctions (such as, *and, as, at, but, by, if, or, to, up*) unless they are the first words in the title.

> I read the chapter "Your Future in a Computer World" in the book TODAY'S MODERN BUSINESS OFFICE.
>
> Pat contributed an article entitled "Comments on Our Grading System" to The Student Record, our school newspaper.

TRY-OUT EXERCISE

Directions: Rekey the following sentences, indicating titles with quotation marks or underscores. In addition, capitalize the most important words in the titles.

1. Today's new york times has an interesting article entitled the world in which we live.
2. For my birthday I received a monthly subscription to the magazine the teen review.
3. Let's make a toast to our teachers is the name of an article that appeared in the square deal, our school paper.
4. The chapter paris at the time of the french revolution was assigned by our history teacher.
5. Have you read the book entitled a tale of two cities?

SENTENCE EXERCISE

Directions: Rekey the following sentences in the spaces provided, supplying quotation marks, commas, capitalization, and underscores wherever necessary. In addition, capitalize the most important words in the titles. If a sentence requires no changes, key *correct* in the space below it.

EXAMPLE:

My mother asked did you clean your room?

My mother asked, "Did you clean your room?"

1. Corianne said I had tuna fish for lunch and enjoyed it.

_____

2. Watch your step on the rocks, warned the guide.

_____

3. Loreen said I am going to join the Army when I graduate; and she did.

_____

4. Our teacher asked who can tell us the author of the book arms and the man?

_____

5. Three people came to my side when I murmured I feel ill: Frank, Pat, and Gil.

_____

6. Don't you see the sign that reads form a single line?

_____

7. I enjoyed reading the article entitled with a song in my heart in the magazine music world.

_____

_____

8. The florist warned you should water this plant every day; but I forgot to do it.

_____

_____

9. My sister says that she wants to become a doctor.

_____

10. You must see this movie, urged the critic in the gazette.

_____

DICTIONARY USAGE

Directions: Here are the more difficult words and their meanings that appear in the assignments in this unit. Study them carefully; complete the sentences that follow.

antique (adjective)	of a bygone style or period
auction (noun)	a public sale at which property or goods are sold to the highest bidder
auctioneer	one who conducts an auction
aware	having knowledge of
bid (verb) (to _____ at an auction)	to offer to buy
caution (verb)	to warn
convey	to communicate; make known
daze (noun)	a stunned or shocked condition
gavel (noun)	a hammerlike tool with a head normally made of wood commonly used by an auctioneer to signal for attention or to confirm a sale
Victorian (adjective)	of or relating to the reign of Queen Victoria of England

Directions for completing the following sentences: Select the appropriate word from the above list, and key it in each blank.

1. After he hit his head in a fall, the boy was in a _____ .
2. The _____ banged his _____ and shouted, "Sold to the lady in the red hat!"
3. Are you _____ that you have been late six times this term?
4. My brother's wife collects _____ Chinese vases from the last century and has just bought another at an _____ .
5. The judge said, "I must _____ you to tell the truth."
6. I bought an old pin that is from the English _____ period.
7. At the auction two people began to _____ on the same painting.
8. Please _____ my best wishes to your parents on their anniversary.
9. I ran to the station but was not _____ that the train had already left.
10. At the musuem I saw an _____ desk that was once owned by George Washington.

HELPFUL-HINT LETTER

Directions: Key this personal-business letter in modified block style with indented paragraphs and open punctuation. Quotation marks are necessary for the following: two direct quotations (insert a comma before the quotation and capitalize the first word) and the title of an article. The title of a magazine also appears. The important words of the two titles must be capitalized.

Use a full sheet of paper.
Margins: 50-space line (elite 26-81; pica 17-72)
Tabs: Elite 31, 51; pica 22, 42
Center points: Elite 51; pica 42

Key your return address at the center of the 13th line from the top edge of the paper; the date is on line 15 under your two-line return address. Quadruple-space after the date, and key the inside address (name and address of person to whom the letter is going). Double-space; key the salutation. Double-space after the salutation, and single-space the body. Double-space after the body; key the complimentary close at the center point. Quadruple-space, and key your name at the center point.

Your street address
Your city, state ZIP
April 15, 19--

Mr. John Velten, Editor
Marden Publications
364 Brisbane Street
Memphis, TN 38104-3720

Dear Mr. Velten

I recently read an article in business daily entitled are students aware of the importance of correct spelling?

My teacher, Mrs. Greco, certainly agrees with the author of the article. She constantly tells us it is important that you spell correctly and use your dictionaries. I showed the article to Mrs. Greco, and she read it aloud to the class. She then turned to me and said perhaps you can obtain copies of this article for everyone; therefore, I am writing to ask for 25 copies if they are available.

Mrs. Greco also asked that I convey to you her thanks for including such an important topic in the magazine.

Sincerely

Your name

Directions: Key the following short report, indicating quotations and titles correctly. Refer to page 5 for a review of proofreader's marks.

Use a full sheet of paper.
Margins: 60-space line (elite 21-86; pica 12-77)
Tabs: Elite 26; pica 17
Center points: Elite 51; pica 42

Center the title on the 12th line from the top edge of the paper for elite and the 10th line for pica. Quadruple-space to the first paragraph. Double-space the report. Indent paragraphs 5 spaces.

NOTE: You will not be able to copy this report line for line. Use your judgment as to where each line should end within the margins given.

Center / *quadruple space*

Sold to the Highest Bidder

I had never been to an auction until my mother saw an advertisment in the daily star announcing an auction of antique furniture. She smiled and said I always wanted a victorian sofa; and we were on our way. My Mother told me that at an auction people bid on the item they wish to purchase; it is sold to the highest bidder. She also cautioned don't raise your hand during the auction because the auctioneer will think that you are bidding. My mother and another lady bid on the same sofa. Finally the other lady stopped bidding. The auctioneer banged his gavel and shouted sold to the highest bidder! My mother had her Victorian sofa. *stet* The next week my mother asked would you like to go to another auction? We now have an arm chair to match the sofa.

Directions: Key this personal note in block style with open punctuation, indicating quotations and titles correctly.

Use a full sheet of paper.
Margins: 60-space line (elite 21-86; pica 12-77)

All parts of the note are to be keyed at the left margin. Key the date on the 15th line from the top edge of the paper. Quadruple-space, and key the salutation. Double-space after the salutation, and single-space the body. Double-space after the body; key the complimentary close.

June 17, 19--

Dear Roberto

I have great news for you. My brother Seth, who is a senior
in high school, is a celebrity. He has just won a national
science award.

You can imagine how excited my family is. I knew he would win
it my father keeps repeating. My mother can't stop saying my
son is a genius. Seth simply walks around in a daze murmuring
I don't believe it!

Our neighbors are constantly ringing our bell to congratulate
Seth. The school paper, the tattletale, featured an article
about him entitled seth puts our town on the map.

I will enclose a copy of the article in my next letter.

Sincerely

CONTEXT CHECK

[What is the
communication about?]

Directions: Following are three groups of sentences concerning the two letters and the report in this unit that you have keyed. Fill in the blanks, or indicate the correct answers as otherwise requested. You may refer to the communications.

HELPFUL-HINT LETTER

1. The article discussed by the writer is entitled _____
   _____ .

2. Does Mrs. Greco agree with the author of the article about the importance of correct spelling?
   Yes _____ No _____

3. Mrs. Greco asked the writer to try to obtain _____ for everyone in the class.

YOU'RE ON YOUR OWN—ASSIGNMENT NO. 1

1. The writer's mother decided to bid on a _____ at the auction.

2. At an auction an item is sold to the _____ bidder.

3. Did the writer's mother bid successfully on the item she wished to purchase?
   Yes _____ No _____

YOU'RE ON YOUR OWN—ASSIGNMENT NO. 2

1. Seth has just won a _____ .

2. Was Seth's father surprised when Seth won it?
   Yes _____ No _____

3. The article in the school newspaper about Seth is entitled _____
   _____ .

PROOFREADING ASSIGNMENT

Directions: Insert proofreader's marks to indicate corrections in the following paragraph. Here are the 6 marks that will have to be inserted.

≡	capitalize	w̲e̲ left early.	We left early.
◡	close up	Din ner is ready.	Dinner is ready.
ℰ	delete	All iss well.	All is well.
#	insert space	We aregoing.	We are going.
∧	insert period	Write soon I'll miss you.	Write soon. I'll miss you.
∾	transpose	enuogh	enough

A visit to the dentist can be a verry trying expereince. I go

for a check-up every six months; however, i would rather be

any where in this world than sitting in the dentist's chair I am

sure that youfeel the same way that I do.

Review Lesson Units 10-12

NAME _____

SENTENCE REVIEW

Directions: Rekey the following sentences in the spaces provided, correcting the troublesome words, expressing the numbers correctly, and indicating titles and quotations.

EXAMPLE:

Antoine asked have you past all your tests?

Antoine asked, "Have you passed all your tests?"

1. The saleslady warned you have only until December 3d to return this coat.

_____

2. At ease, said the captain as he past the private with her arm rised in a salute.

_____

3. I was sure surprised to learn that a ninety-story building will raise on that site.

_____

4. The sign in the library read no food allowed; but my friend ate her lunch.

_____

5. The article I wrote for the school paper was entitled exploring the past can be fun!

_____

6. The dentist asked how many times a day do you brush?

_____

7. Millie said that she could not choose between the blue hat for $15.00 and the red one for nine dollars.

_____

8. Come by my house for lunch on the 15 of August, said Magda.

_____

9. My doctor advised you should walk 3 miles daily but I'm too lazy.

_____

_____

10. I read the article entitled recent graduate tells of his climb to success, which appeared in the magazine a business viewpoint.

_____

_____

11. There were 4 students in the room when the teacher announced the test is now over: Art, Louise, Harry, and Milt.

_____

_____

12. 300 people each pledged ten dollars to the charity; less than 15 didn't pay.

_____

_____

13. Jerry said I am real anxious to have pecan pie for dessert; but the waitress brought ice cream instead.

_____

_____

14. Did you hear the waitress say sir, we are out of pecan pie?

_____

15. By the 22 of September, 19 boys and eleven girls had paid their club dues.

_____

Directions: Key this personal note in modified block style with mixed punctuation. Use a full sheet of paper with a 60-space line. Wherever necessary, correct the troublesome words, express the numbers correctly, and indicate titles and quotations.

NOTE: You will not be able to copy this letter exactly as it appears. Use your judgment as to where each line should end within the margins.

May 19, 19--

Dear Hector:

On the 11 of May, our class went by the library with our teacher, Ms. Mapes, who is real anxious for us to begin thinking about careers. The day before she had instructed list 3 occupations you would like to research.

22 students are in my class. The librarian, Mr. Kay, greeted us. He said I will leave each of you borrow 2 books; and he showed us around. As we past one shelf, he pointed out reference books that we could examine.

Mr. Kay told us that he had been a librarian for eighteen years and enjoyed his work. He advised us to make up our minds soon about a career and asked are you aware that time flies?

Hector, choosing a career is surely difficult.

Sincerely,

Directions: Key this personal-business letter in block style with open punctuation. Use a full sheet of paper with a 60-space line. Wherever necessary, correct the troublesome words, express the numbers correctly, and indicate titles and quotations.

NOTE: You will not be able to copy this letter exactly as it appears. Use your judgment as to where each line should end within the margins.

Your street address
Your city, state ZIP
October 29, 19--

Mr. Walter Rebhun, President
Rebhun Publishing Company
1180 Boynton Avenue
Baton Rouge, LA 70802-2980

Dear Mr. Rebhun

On weekends I wait on tables in my parents' restaurant. I
sleep less hours than most of my friends because I wake up
when the sun raises. However, I really don't mind because
some real interesting people come by the restaurant.

We were recently written up in your newspaper, the star gazette.
The article was entitled dining on superb food but at reason-
able prices, and it brought us about 50 new customers. Last
Saturday, the 22 of October, 8 people came in for lunch. One
of the men said young man, we are celebrating the signing of
a new contract; and he proceeded to order the most expensive
items on the menu. When the man paid the bill, he left me a
tip of twenty dollars.

Thank you for your complimentary article.

Sincerely

Your name

PROOFREADING REVIEW

Directions: Insert proofreader's marks to indicate corrections in the following paragraph. Here are the 6 marks that will have to be inserted.

Mark	Meaning	Example	Corrected
☰	capitalize	i may go.	I may go.
◡	close up	over whelm	overwhelm
∧	insert	Be carful.	Be careful.
# ∧	insert space	Don'tleave.	Don't leave.
/	lowercase letter	I'm Sorry.	I'm sorry.
⌐	move left	I don't agree with you.	I don't agree with you.

My brother andI enjoy camping. We especialy like sleeping

out doors. there's nothing like sleeping under a blanket of

        stars. There are no city noises; the rustle of the Trees

is the loudest noise that we hear.

THE FOLLOWING PAGES CONTAIN THE

REFERENCE GUIDE

ILLUSTRATION 1 - PERSONAL NOTE IN BLOCK STYLE WITH OPEN PUNCTUATION

```
February 23, 19--


Dear Norman

During the past week, we had a terrible storm.

Twelve inches of snow fell, and the winds blew down several
trees.  Ice and snow was all around our house.  However, my
brother Hank managed to dig a path to the road.  Our neigh-
bors, the Brill family, had no electricity for a few hours.
My father loaned them a flashlight, candles, and blankets.
School was closed for one day.

The storm lasted for about eight hours.  Norman, we were happy
when it was over.

Sincerely
```

ILLUSTRATION 2 - PERSONAL NOTE IN MODIFIED BLOCK STYLE WITH MIXED PUNCTUATION

July 18, 19--

Dear Billy:

I enjoyed being your guest while visiting St. Louis,
Missouri, last week. During our two hours together,
I especially enjoyed seeing your garden. It is so
beautiful.

You have so many different varieties of flowers; it
is hard to choose a favorite. The garden is a mass
of colors; one sees yellow, red, purple, blue, pink,
orange, and white. As I told you at the time, Billy,
there is a feeling of peace.

I will write to you the next time we visit St. Louis
and hope to be able to visit you again.

Sincerely,

ILLUSTRATION 3 - SHORT REPORT

MOUNT ST. HELENS

On a quiet Sunday in May of 1980, Mount St. Helens
erupted. Cars, trucks, buses, trains, and planes stopped.
All normal activity ceased, and people tried to find their
way home.

Mount St. Helens is located in the state of Washington,
but the winds blew the ash from the volcano over other states
as well. Skies darkened in cities as far away as 85 miles,
and a covering of ash fell on everyone and everything. At
the site of the volcano, scalding gases and hot debris traveled at 200 miles an hour. A blanket of ash fell over the
ruins. A number of people were killed, wildlife was destroyed,
and trees were uprooted.

We all hope that Mount St. Helens will not erupt again.

ILLUSTRATION 4 - PERSONAL-BUSINESS LETTER IN BLOCK STYLE WITH OPEN PUNCTUATION

```
Your street address
Your city, state  ZIP
April 23, 19--


Miss Toshi Nozaki
ENERGY MAGAZINE
9 East Clark Street
Dallas, TX  75229-6218

Dear Miss Nozaki

Because of this country's energy shortage, our
science teacher gave our class the assignment of
writing about sources of energy other than oil.

My classmates are writing on obtaining energy
from coal, waterpower, and wind.  I considered
the problem and decided to write on solar energy.
The sun is always with me, and I think that its
heat will be an important future source of energy.

If you have any books, booklets, or magazine arti-
cles on solar energy, I would appreciate receiv-
ing them.  When I finish reading them, I will
return them to you immediately.

Cordially yours


Your name
```

Your street address
Your city, state ZIP
March 16, 19--

Mr. Lung Shen
Modern Clothing Shoppe
360 Brisbane Street
Memphis, TN 38104-0351

Dear Mr. Shen:

You may have read in the newspaper that there was a fire in
the Bailey home this past week; unfortunately, all the Baileys'
possessions were destroyed. Therefore, our class is asking for
storekeepers' help for the Baileys; and we hope that you'll
make a donation.

You can donate either cash or clothing--whichever is better
for you. The three Bailey children's clothing sizes are as
follows: 10, 12, and 16. All are girls.

If you wish to make a donation, please send it to me; or I can
pick it up after 3:00 p.m. Give whatever you can; the Baileys
will appreciate it.

Sincerely,

Your name
Class Representative

Your street address
Your city, state ZIP
April 23, 19--

Mr. Robert Cooper, President
Cooper Brothers, Inc.
1025 Ascot Street
Hackensack, NJ 07601-1675

Dear Mr. Cooper

    I went to your store three weeks ago and pur-
chased a doll as a birthday gift for my younger
sister.

    The doll lay in its box for a month until yes-
terday when I gave it to my sister. Its arms and
legs are supposed to be movable; we were very upset
when we could not raise the doll's right arm.

    I stopped at the store this morning, but the
manager would not let me return the doll because I
had purchased it more than three weeks ago. However,
it had been lying in its box and was surely never
used.

    If you will not exchange it, please advise me if
you will repair the doll's arm so that it can be raised.

Sincerely yours

Your name

Index

A

B

C

D

E

F

G

H

I

L

M

Modified block style, personal-business letter in, with mixed punctuation, 149; personal-business letter in, with indented paragraphs and open punctuation, 150; personal note with mixed punctuation, 146

Money, expressed as numbers, 120

N

Neither, nor, 14

Newspapers, titles of, 3

Note, *See* Personal note

Nouns, proper, 1; using apostrophe with: plural, ending in *S*, 83; plural, not ending in *S*, 84; singular, 83

Numbers, 119-128; at sentence beginning, 120; dates in, 120; expressed, 119; indefinite amounts, 119; money in, 120

O

Open punctuation, personal-business letter in block style with, 148; personal-business letter in modified block style with indented paragraphs and, 150; personal note in block style with, 145

P

parenthetical expressions, defined, 47; commas used with, 47

Passed, past, use of, 109

Personal-business letter: block style with open punctuation, 148; modified block style with indented paragraphs and open punctuation, 150; modified block sytle with mixed punctuation, 149

Personal note, block style with open punctuation, 145; modified block style with mixed punctuation, 146

Personal pronouns, 23-31; after preposition, 24; after verb, *to be*, 24; two subjects joined by *and*, 23

Plural subjects, and singular, 13

Possession: plural nouns ending in *S*, 83; plural nouns not ending in *S*, 84; singular nouns and, 83; using apostrophe with, 83-92

Preposition, personal pronoun after, 24

Pronouns, personal, 23-31; after preposition, 24; after verb, *to be*, 24; two subjects joined by *and*, 23

Proofreader's marks, review of, 5

Q

Question marks, used with quotation marks, 129

Quotation marks, 129-138; with colons and semicolons, 130; with commas, 130; with direct quotations, 129; with exclamation points, 130; with publication titles, 131; with question marks, 130

R

Raise, rise, use of, 110; principal parts of, 110

Real, very, use of, 110

Reference guide, 145

Report, short, 147

S

Salutation, capitalization of, 4

Seasons, capitalization of, 3

Semicolon, before transitional word or phrase, 72; between independent clauses, 71; colon and, 71-82; to replace connecting word, 72; used with quotation marks, 130

Series, commas used with, 57

Singular, plural subjects and, 13

Singular cases, special, 15

Subject and verb agreement, 13-22

Subjects, separated from verbs, 14; singular and plural, 13

Sure, surely, use of, 111

T

To, use of with *at, by*, 111

To Be, personal pronoun after, 24

Titles, books, 3; magazine, 3; newspaper, 3; personal, 2; use of quotation marks in publication, 131

V

Verb, agreement of subject and, 13-22; separated from subject, 14

Very, real, use of, 110